ENJOY LIFE'S™

cookies for
everyone!

ENJOY LIFE'S™ cookies for everyone!

150 DELICIOUS GLUTEN-FREE TREATS THAT ARE SAFE FOR MOST ANYONE WITH FOOD ALLERGIES, INTOLERANCES, OR SENSITIVITIES

LESLIE HAMMOND AND BETSY LAAKSO

FAIR WINDS
PRESS
BEVERLY, MASSACHUSETTS

Text © 2009 Leslie Hammond

First published in the USA in 2009 by
Fair Winds Press, a member of
Quayside Publishing Group
100 Cummings Center
Suite 406-L
Beverly, MA 01915-6101
www.fairwindspress.com

13 12 11 10 09   1 2 3 4 5

ISBN-13: 978-1-59233-369-1
ISBN-10: 1-59233-369-9

Library of Congress Cataloging-in-Publication Data
Hammond, Leslie.
  Enjoy life's cookies for everyone! : 150 delicious gluten-free treats
that are safe for most anyone with food allergies, intolerances, and
sensitivities / Leslie Hammond.
     p. cm.
  ISBN-13: 978-1-59233-369-1
  ISBN-10: 1-59233-369-9
  1. Food allergy--Diet therapy--Recipes. 2. Cookies. I. Title.
  RC588.D53H35 2009
  641.5'631--dc22
                      2008052254

Cover design and book design: Kathie Alexander
Photography: Darin Ashton, Ashton Photography

Printed and bound in Singapore

To my three amazing little girls,
Wendy, Allison, and Madeline

Contents

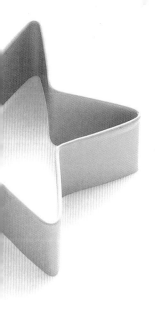

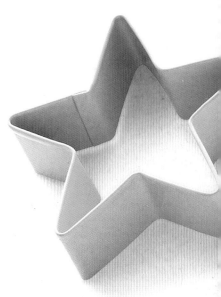

Foreword

At Enjoy Life®, our whole business is making smile-good foods that keep people's insides happy too.

When I started Enjoy Life Foods in 2001, I had a mission of making great-tasting allergy-friendly and gluten-free foods that most everyone can eat freely. Since then, our mission has remained constant—all of our products are specially made to be free of the eight most common allergens (no wheat, dairy, peanuts, tree nuts, eggs, soy, fish, or shellfish) AND gluten-free. Early on, we also made the decision that we would make all of our products in a dedicated nut- and gluten-free facility for customers' safety and peace of mind. Our Enjoy Life product line has now expanded to include cookies, snack bars, cereals, granolas, bagels, trail mixes, chocolate chips, and chocolate bars . . . and we're introducing new foods all the time. If you want to learn more, visit us at www.enjoylifefoods.com.

I am not personally affected by food allergies or intolerances; however, many members of the Enjoy Life team are, and so we *all* have a deep understanding and appreciation for how challenging and (sometimes) frustrating it can be to find delicious and nutritious foods when you have dietary restrictions.

At Enjoy Life, we want to help people "enjoy life" by offering delicious, healthy, and, most importantly, safe foods that nearly everyone can enjoy even if they have food allergies, food intolerances, Celiac Disease, autism, or other health concerns. Food is central to our culture and way of life, and we never want anyone to miss out on life's little pleasures just because they can't eat certain foods.

There is nothing more satisfying to me personally than when a mother, for example, tells me that our cookies help make her food-allergic son feel more "normal" and included when his classmates are eating their after-school treats . . . or when I see the grin on a little girl's face as she eats a chocolate bar for the very first time . . . or when I talk to a dad who tells me that our foods have taken some of the worry and anxiety out of feeding his child . . . or when an adult gets diagnosed with Celiac Disease and discovers a whole new world of delicious gluten-free foods that make her feel good. These moments and your gratitude and appreciation for what we do motivate and inspire all of us at Enjoy Life each and every day.

When Fair Winds Press and Leslie Hammond first approached us about partnering on an allergy-friendly cookie cookbook, we got very excited about the project. What could be better than creating a cookbook full of 150 cookie recipes that are free of the eight most common allergens, easy to make, and really tasty? Thanks to this unique cookbook, there's no need to worry about whether the recipes are safe or whether they will turn out well—Leslie and her family have multiple food allergies themselves, so she is very familiar with the challenges of baking allergy-friendly treats. Plus, you can rest assured that the Enjoy Life team has reviewed each and every recipe in the book to make sure they are safe, healthy, and, most importantly, totally delicious!

We hope that this cookbook helps you and your family "enjoy life" in the kitchen and beyond.

Wishing you happy and healthy eating.

Scott B. Mandell
CEO, President, and Founder
Enjoy Life Foods
smandell@enjoylifenb.com

Introduction

What Happens when the Cookies You Love Are the Treats You Can't Eat?

The conventional ingredients in our favorite baked goods make them look, taste, and smell irresistible. Wheat flour makes the cookie soft and chewy. Creamy butter and eggs give a rich taste and weight on the tongue. Chocolate, white chocolate, butterscotch, candies, and nuts give cookies a kick that excites our taste buds.

Now, imagine being allergic to all of these ingredients.

However, having to avoid many allergens does not mean having to sacrifice your favorite treats. With 150 delicious recipes that are gluten-free, wheat-free, peanut-free, dairy-free, egg-free, treenut-free, fish- and shellfish-free, and soy-free, this cookbook will allow you to have your cookies and eat them too! What's more, the recipes are yummy and simple to make. *Cookies for Everyone!* is packed full of helpful information, family stories, tricks of the trade, and love.

Life without the Cookie.

Without staple ingredients like eggs, dairy, butter, and wheat flour, what do you do to indulge in the occasional treat? Even more challenging—what do you do for your children when they want to have the same treat that everyone else is enjoying? Is it possible to make delicious cookies without the wheat flour, eggs, soy, nuts, and/or dairy? Or, better yet, can you make a desirable, chewy, melt-in-your-mouth cookie that your kids will actually approve of?

DID YOU KNOW?
Food allergies affect 12 million Americans, or 4 percent of the population. More than 6.5 million Americans are allergic to seafood, and over 3 million are allergic to peanuts and tree nuts.
(Source: Food Allergy Initiative)

I had the experience of being the kid who couldn't eat anything. I know the feeling of watching everyone else enjoying tasty treats while I sat on the sidelines during birthday parties and holidays. There were no mouthwatering gingerbread men at Christmas, decorated sugar cookies at Easter, Halloween, or Valentine's Day, or even a warm chocolate chip cookie with a glass of cold milk at bedtime.

Now, I am the mom of three little girls who all have a variety of foods they have to avoid. So between the four of us we stay away from gluten, dairy, tree nuts, and soy. Our food restrictions vary, so not all of us have to avoid each ingredient. So do I make four different cookies for each of us, or one awesome cookie to suit all of our needs? My years of cooking experience have proven you can make a cookie that everyone can eat and that everyone will love.

About This Cookbook

This cookbook is all about allergy-friendly cookies. Keep in mind that even though you have allergies, there are many foods, such as whole grains, lean meats, fruits, and vegetables that provide the nutrients that you need. Cookies are cookies, allergy-friendly or not. They are not the mainstay of our diet, but a special tasty treat. Many of my cookie recipes call for healthy flours and ingredients that provide nutrients and fiber—which allows you to sneak some good stuff to your family in the form of a treat! Of course, a few of the recipes are just simply delicious little sugary fun GOODIES! To get the bulk of your nutrients, stick to the healthy stuff. Then, after your nutritious meal, have a cookie!

Parents who cook allergy-friendly for their families have told me that, most of all, they simply want a cookbook that focuses on the eight major food allergies as defined in the United States (wheat, dairy, egg, soy, tree nuts, peanuts, fish, and shellfish). No variations or substitutions, not a book that just focuses on one or two allergens, but a clear, easy-to-follow book that is dedicated to avoiding every one of the eight major allergens.

So here you go! All 150 cookies recipes are gluten-, wheat-, dairy-, egg-, soy-, tree nut-, and peanut-free. Of course, there are no shellfish or fish in these yummy cookies, but as easy as it would seem to avoid fish in cookies, many products are contaminated with seafood, so we do avoid those potential risks. These recipes are easy to follow and precise. I give options for corn-, sulfite-, and potato-free variations for those who have problems with those ingredients. For example, powdered sugar contains cornstarch, so I teach you how to make corn-free powdered sugar. Egg replacer often contains potato starch, so I show you how to make your own egg replacement.

With those few exceptions, the other recipes cater to your needs without variations. "Well, what if I am only allergic to dairy, gluten, and nuts, but can have eggs?" you ask. Should you just add an egg to the batter? Nope! The recipes are designed to be free of the big eight food allergens. Each recipe is formulated with a combination of ingredients to mimic the allergenic ingredients and is designed to taste good as it is. There is no need to add an egg even if you can eat them. In fact, adding an egg might change the chemistry of the baked good, for example, and throw it off.

Taking Minimal Ingredients and Making the Most of Them!

Let's look at some of the ingredients that we are working with—rice flour, tapioca flour, flax meal, oils, sugars, fruits, and allergy-friendly chocolates, to name a few. My goal, much like yours, is to give ourselves and our families a goody that mimics what others are having, to put a smile on our faces from having a treat that we can eat, and to share it with friends who will like it too!

Most of us have experienced that sometimes a purchased or homemade allergy-friendly food doesn't taste or shape together exactly like the foods that are made with regular ingredients, like goodies made with wheat flour, butter, and eggs. Consider that most of these recipes also don't use margarine, potato flour, or corn flour/starch, which really aid in the texture, taste, and shape of cookies in allergy-friendly baking. If you are allergic to a combination of these ingredients, then you know the challenges of baking without them! It is also hard to find products and recipes that are free of all eight major allergens as well as corn, potato, and sulfites! Enter creativity! With limited ingredients we have to find alternative techniques and substitutions. For example, several of my recipes call for powdered sugar, which contains cornstarch. If you are not allergic to corn, feel free to use regular powdered sugar. If you are allergic to corn, however, I give a delicious alternative recipe to make your own corn-free version.

It was my goal to create cookies that were buttery, light, and tasty that also looked like your usual cookie even though they were made with "unusual" ingredients. I am very pleased with these cookies. For such limited ingredients, I think that they turned out really well. My tasters were happy too!

A FAMILY DISCOVERS NEW TASTES AND NEW OUTLOOK

Erika Hastings

When my daughter was first born, she had a runny nose all throughout the winter. Being a first-time parent I thought that was normal, until springtime hit and then I thought, "How could she have a cold for four months straight? Something's not right." At the same time I started putting the pieces together that whenever I would eat certain foods, it would go through to my breast milk and my daughter would throw up from it. And so I began the journey to discovering her food allergies.

Since I was still breastfeeding her, everything that she was allergic to, I also had to avoid or else it would make her sick. And this meant learning a lot of new food tricks and also practicing some serious self-discipline as I gave up a lot of my favorite foods and searched for comforting, delicious replacements. I relied on the Internet a lot in the beginning as I looked for new recipes and new ways of cooking. I stocked up on new cookbooks and did a lot of experimentation. Some things worked, and some things went straight to the garbage! I started up a parenting blog and posted some of my recipe experiments on it to be able to share with others (www.mudspice.wordpress.com). One of the big challenges I had was learning where to buy all of the strange new ingredients that I had never

seen or heard of before. It took a lot of searching around at various natural food stores, but now I know just where to go and what to get. It's always a thrill whenever I discover new, delicious foods at the stores with things that we can all eat.

Two years later when my son was born, his allergies were even more severe, but this time I was able to figure out most of them within his first few weeks of life. Now that I am pregnant with my third child, I am trying to avoid all of the main allergy foods that my other two kids had, because in my research I learned that if those foods are avoided during pregnancy, there is a possibility of decreasing the newborn baby's allergies. We'll see if it works!

I've found that it's taken me several years to change my adult taste buds to actually enjoy the alternative foods that I have to make for the allergies my kids have. I found that the most helpful thing for me was finding good comfort food replacements, especially sweets and desserts. My kids, on the other hand, since they have grown up eating this way, actually prefer their rice bread, soy cheese, and chickpea flour muffins to any of the other wheat and dairy options that they have occasionally tasted!

U.S. FOOD LABELING

A U.S. food labeling law now requires food manufacturers to disclose in plain language whether products contain any of the top eight food allergens. The Food Allergen Labeling and Consumer Protection Act (FALCPA), which took effect January 1, 2006, mandates that foods containing milk, eggs, fish, crustacean shellfish, peanuts, tree nuts, wheat, and soy must declare the food in plain language on the ingredient list or via the word "Contains" followed by the name of the major food allergen (milk, wheat, or eggs for example) or a parenthetical statement in the list of ingredients [e.g., "albumin (egg)"]. Such ingredients must be listed even if they are present in colors, flavors, or spice blends. Additionally, manufacturers must list the specific nut or seafood that is used (e.g., almond, walnut, cashew; or tuna, salmon, shrimp, or lobster). While more than 160 foods have been identified as causing allergic reactions, the eight foods listed above cause 90 percent of food-allergic reactions in the U.S.

FALCPA will certainly make label-reading easier for the millions of Americans living with food allergies. However, not all companies do a good job of identifying allergens. Contact the FDA if you find a food product that is mislabeled or is not clear. Food packaged to order and restaurants are not required to have ingredient statements, so use caution when eating foods without FALCPA-compliant labels. Learn more at: www.foodallergy.org/Advocacy/labeling.html.

What Are the Most Common Allergens?

In the United States, eight foods ("the big eight") account for 90 percent of all food-allergic reactions. According to the U.S. Food and Drug Administration (FDA), the most common food allergens are wheat, dairy, peanuts, tree nuts, egg, soy, fish, and shellfish. These eight common allergens are now required to be clearly labeled on all packaged food products in the United States according to the Food Allergen Labeling and Consumer Protection Act (FALCPA).

In Canada, they recognize *ten* common allergens—those listed above, plus sesame and sulfites. The good news is that all the recipes in this allergy-friendly cookbook are free of all ten allergens!

Everyone Has Different Tastes!

Take a Snickerdoodle, for example. Traditional Snickerdoodles are slightly crunchy on the outside, soft in the center, rich and buttery, and hold their round shape. I will be honest—I make great gluten-free Snickerdoodles, and many people have told me that they are better than the wheat version. But my original recipe still contained eggs and dairy. It is amazing how one little ingredient, like the egg, can play such a huge role in the taste, texture, and shaping of the cookie. Thankfully, there are allergy-friendly ingredients that can mimic the function of allergenic ingredients like eggs, and I have experimented to find the best, most delicious substitutions. In these recipes, I have turned to allergy-friendly ingredients like flax meal and applesauce to help maintain the taste, texture, and shape of the cookie.

Some people like allergy-friendly cookies even more than the regular ones, and some have a hard time with the taste or texture. Everyone's tastes vary. I can make a cookie that I do not like, and my Grandpa will eat it with joy and ask for more. I can make a decadent, amazing, allergy-friendly brownie that I love, and some people might think it is too sweet. We all have different tastes and may not like every single cookie that we try, but with 150 recipes to choose from, I am sure you will be able to find your favorite allergy-friendly cookies in this book. I offer a large variety of cookies, bars, no/added/sugar treats, and handheld goodies that will delight many different taste buds! Try one of the cookie recipes made with just the rice and tapioca flour and compare it with one with the sorghum and flax meal bases. There is something for everyone, cookies we can all eat. It is up to you and your family to pick which ones fit you best. Enjoy!

Chapter 1

Benefits of Alternative Eating

Limiting your foods can make eating challenging.
You find yourself spending more time in the kitchen,
reading more labels, and eating out less. The downside
is that you can't rely on fast foods or packaged foods,
but these are often low in nutrition and high in fat and
calories. The fact is that even though you can't eat
gluten, dairy, nuts, soy, eggs, etc., there are so many
delicious and nutritious fresh foods that you can enjoy.
So on the bright side, having food allergies compels you
to eat fresher, which is healthier for you!

Knowledge Is Power

Having awareness of what we put into our bodies can be a blessing in disguise! I find that my children have a healthier advantage in society because they have to learn how to make responsible food choices. They are very aware of foods they can and cannot have. They understand the concept at an early age that certain foods are not good for their bodies. I see that this helps them relate to health in an easier way. Much like how wheat can hurt their tummies, they can relate to the concept that too much sugar makes their bodies feel "icky" and is not always good for them.

Another plus is that we spend time as a family together preparing our meals and talking about nutrition and our bodies. My kids love cooking and creating with me in the kitchen. With today's statistics of overweight and unhealthy kids, at times I am pleased that there are foods we have to avoid because it makes us more aware of the link between food and health. I also find that many allergy-friendly foods are made from natural and organic ingredients. That's better for us and our earth.

Whether you have food allergies or not, one benefit of eating a limited diet is that you know what's in your food—because you made it! You have more control over how much sugar you use, you can use as many organic ingredients as possible, avoid added preservatives, and use natural products. Plus, you get to have the benefit of licking the beaters and having delicious smells in the kitchen as your foods bake in the oven!

Although cookies are not meant to be your main source of nutrition, I do want to highlight how these homemade cookies are better for you than many purchased cookies. Preservatives, chemicals, possible contamination, high sugars, and corn syrup (just to mention a few) are some things that might lurk in purchased cookies. Also, many purchased cookies contain one or more of the big eight food allergens. I often find cookies that are gluten- and egg-free, but not dairy- and soy-free as well. Rest assured that all of these cookies avoid the eight major US food allergens (wheat, dairy, egg, soy, tree nuts, peanuts, fish, and shellfish) plus gluten.

Avoiding Wheat/Gluten

Going wheat- or gluten-free is a great opportunity to increase whole food variety in your diet. Whole grains don't have to be all about wheat! Many other grains are full of helpful nutrients. All of these grains are included in this cookbook:

- **Millet**—Exceptionally nutritious and rich in protein, phosphorus, B vitamins, and iron.
- **Quinoa**—One cup (185g) of quinoa has more calcium than a quart (1.1L) of milk and twice the protein of barley or rice. It is a good complement to legumes that are often low in the amino acid methionine, and it is higher in oil than other grains.
- **Certified Gluten-Free Oats**—A good source of the B vitamins thiamin, niacin, and riboflavin. They also provide iron, protein, and fiber.
- **Flax**—Flaxseeds contain a high-quality protein and are rich in soluble fiber. Flax seeds contain vitamins B1, B2, C, E, and carotene. These seeds also contain iron, zinc, and trace amounts of potassium, magnesium, phosphorus, calcium, and vitamin E and carotene, two nutrients that aid the metabolism of the oil. Flaxseeds contain over a hundred times more of a phytonutrient called lignans than any of its closest competitors, such as wheat bran.
- **Buckwheat**—Relatively low in calories and an excellent source of protein, complex carbohydrates, fiber, and magnesium.

How Common Is Celiac Disease?

Once thought to be a rare disorder, Celiac Disease is now estimated to affect 1 in 100 Americans. Symptoms of the disease vary widely in nature, depending on the individual. While Celiac Disease remains one of the most under-diagnosed health conditions today, the good news is that increasing awareness of the disease among patients and health care practitioners has resulted in higher diagnosis rates. For a list of Celiac Disease resources, see Chapter 9.

Many people have noticed healthful benefits to eliminating wheat from their diets, even if they don't have Celiac Disease. Some people have reported relief from constipation, less bloating, and weight loss. Many disorders, diets, and diseases may benefit from restricting gluten in the diet, such as autism, ADHD, SCD, the blood type diet, fibromyalgia, type 1 diabetes, multiple sclerosis, Candida, and dermatitis herpetiformis.

TIP

Genetic Information Non-discrimination Act (GINA)

On May 21, 2008, President Bush signed into law the Genetic Information Nondiscrimination Act (GINA). The new law, which has been called "the first civil rights law of the 21st Century," would prohibit discrimination against individuals on the basis of their genetic information in both employment and health care. This legislation is vital to all individuals who have, or whose family members may have, a genetic condition such as Celiac Disease.

No Dairy

Just because you can't drink milk doesn't mean you'll never have a cool, creamy beverage with your freshly baked cookies. There are many great-tasting fortified alternative beverages on the market with as many or more vitamins as milk. Gluten-free rice beverage is my family's favorite. I prefer the original flavor because it is less sweet. Depending on your allergies, you may find other alternatives like hemp milk to work quite nicely as well. Make sure to read your labels because soy and nuts often are found in alternative milk beverages.

Need calcium? The truth is that calcium is naturally abundant in a wide variety of foods, including most vegetables, fruits, and seeds. In fact, many green vegetables such as broccoli, bok choy, and kale have calcium absorption rates of 50–70 percent—much higher than the 32 percent calcium absorption rate of milk. Many of my cookie recipes include fruits and seeds, but not green vegetables. If you are concerned about your child's calcium consumption, talk to his doctor about purchased calcium powders that you can add to foods, including these cookie recipes.

Whether or not dairy is good for you is a controversial subject. An interesting reason to join the dairy-free movement is that avoiding dairy/casein may be helpful in dealing with autism. The gluten-free/casein-free diet is becoming a mainstream recommendation for the treatment of autism, primarily due to its high success rate and relatively low risk of side effects.

Egg Free

Eggs are a good source of protein, but 70 percent of their calories come from fat. Instead of eggs, try adding ½ cup (86 g) quinoa or (60 g) buckwheat flour, which are high in protein, to your foods. Or ask your doctor/allergist for a rice protein powder that might be acceptable to use in small amounts in your cooking mixtures. This added nutrient should be for a child who eats very little protein and is allergic to eggs and/or is a very picky eater who doesn't get a well balanced diet.

One benefit to avoiding eggs is less exposure to salmonella. The Centers for Disease Control and Prevention estimates there are 76 million instances of foodborne illness and more than 5,000 food-related deaths annually in the United States. Each year there are more than a million salmonella-related cases of food poisoning. Since we are not using eggs, go ahead and lick your spoons and taste the batter—no worries of salmonella contamination here!

Organic Tips

The more you learn about the organic movement, the more it might sway you want to go organic. Not only do organic foods taste better, they are better for you, your children, and our planet. Here are some helpful hints to keep in mind when you buy organic foods.

CERTIFIED ORGANIC LABEL GUIDE
Single-Ingredient Foods

On foods like fruits and vegetables, look for a small sticker version of the USDA Organic label or check the signage in your produce section for this seal. The word "organic" and the seal may also appear on packages of meat, cartons of milk or eggs, cheese.

Multi-Ingredient Foods

Foods such as beverages, snacks, and other processed foods use the following classification system to indicate their use of organic ingredients.

- **100% Organic**—Foods bearing this label are made with 100 percent organic ingredients and may display the USDA Organic seal.
- **Organic**—These products contain at least 95–99 percent organic ingredients (by weight). The remaining ingredients are not available organically but have been approved by the National Organic Program (NOP). These products may display the USDA Organic seal.
- **Made with Organic Ingredients**—Food packaging that reads "Made with Organic Ingredients" must contain 94 percent organic ingredients. These products will not bear the USDA Organic seal; instead, they may list up to three organic ingredients on the front of the packaging.
- **Other**—Products with less than 70 percent organic ingredients may only list organic ingredients on the information panel of the packaging. These products will not bear the USDA Organic seal.

Keep in mind that even if a producer is certified organic, the use of the USDA Organic label is voluntary. At the same time, not everyone goes through the rigorous process of becoming certified, especially smaller farming operations. When shopping at a farmers' market, for example, don't hesitate to ask the vendors how your food was grown. —From www.Organic.org

TIP

Top 10 Foods to Buy Organic
Baby Food
Strawberries *
Rice*
Certified gluten-free rolled oats and other grains*
Milk
Corn*
Bananas*
Green Beans
Peaches*
Apples*

Other produce you should buy organic:
bell peppers
spinach
cherries*
Mexican cantaloupe
celery
sulfite-free apricots*.

*Ingredients found in this cookbook that you should look for in organic varieties.

FOOD ALLERGIES CAN TEACH HARD, BUT REWARDING, LESSONS

Gina Clowes

When my husband and I decided to have kids, I knew I would go back to work. I was one of those women who sneered at stay-home moms because "Motherhood is a relationship, not a career!"

I did end up going back after my first son was born, albeit part-time. I had a terrific job, an adorable son, excellent childcare (Grandma) and a meticulously clean house. After a few years, my husband and I felt another child would complete our family. Since moms are often more relaxed and experience the second time around, I looked forward to an easy time where I'd do an even better job as a parent now that I knew the ropes. I'm sure that somebody up there somewhere got a chuckle out of our assumption that we could improve on the perfection of the first.

After my second son was born, the option of returning to work immediately evaporated, and so did the option of sleeping more than three consecutive hours. My newborn son - who was supposed to be the "easy" one — was covered with head-to-toe hives on his second day of life and those hives stayed with him for years. The pediatrician joked that he had a "face that only a mother could love." When we brought him home from the hospital, he also had terrible acid reflux and we could not lay him down for fear that he would choke on his vomit. It was frightening, and there was no parenting book or motherly advice that was going to make it go away. We changed his diaper for 2 $\frac{1}{2}$ years with his head propped up on pillows.

His first year of life was a whirlwind of acid reflux, eczema, hives, ear infections, and lack of sleep. The pediatrician said he'd grow out of the acid reflux. She told me to count how many times he spit up in a day. I stopped counting after eight times in 30 minutes. For his first 15 months, I slept sitting up in my bed with my son lying face down on my chest.

Confirming a Food Allergy Diagnosis

Every chance I got, I'd jump online to earn a few more credits toward my Google MD. I learned words like atopic dermatitis and urticaria and immunoglobulin E (IgE). After discussing this with my real doctor, she suggested I avoid dairy, then soy, then egg, then wheat, but still things were not better. Of course I was eating peanut butter rice cakes and munching on pistachios for protein. We did allergy skin testing and it was negative. (I later learned that infant skin sometimes does not contain enough mast cells to show a reaction.)

After numerous doctor appointments and conflicting diagnoses, we packed up our family and drove nine hours to New York City to the Jaffe Food Allergy Clinic at Mount Sinai School of Medicine. There, we were able to see one of the leading pediatric allergists in the country. I was hoping he would tell me I was just an anxious mom. But instead he confirmed that our son had over a dozen food allergies, some life threatening. He told us our son should never be without epinephrine. That was the beginning.

The doctor explained that since I was breastfeeding, I had to avoid all the foods to which he was allergic, including milk, wheat, egg, peanuts, tree nuts, sesame, garlic, banana, and more. It wasn't easy, but unlike any reducing diet I'd ever gone on (and gone right back off), this one was for my son. Cheating was not an option.

The good news is that I fit into my jeans from college. The bad news is that I was so cranky, tired, and miserable that no one wanted to be around me.

It was very difficult to go to parties or bunko or even out to dinner. I avoided so many foods that I'd really long for what others were eating. I knew that I was only on the diet for a limited time (6 months), while my son would be on this diet indefinitely. It was only the first glimpse at how challenging his life would become.

Support from Friends and Family
As we shared the news of my son's food allergies with friends and family, we naively assumed that they would rush to learn as much as possible and do whatever they could to accommodate

him. Many pleasantly surprised us, but others really learned enough to gain our confidence.

The pressure and stress that this invisible condition creates can affect everyone in the family. It is so important to get support from family and friends but also from other allergy moms and dads. There is a comradery there and an understanding that those outside the "allergy world" will never get. The exclusion and isolation that can occur is often just as difficult as managing the special foods and the potential for anaphylaxis.

Any mom can tell you that there is no greater pain in life than seeing your child hurt, physically or emotionally. Yet sometimes getting roughed up a little in life brings out the best in us and our kids too. We empathize with our son, but we teach him that food allergies won't stop him from being every thing he was meant to be.

So this story ends with me back at work, but this time I don't need to leave the house. I now facilitate a local support group and am active in food allergy advocacy. I have an online support group with thousands of members worldwide, and I have just published a children's book. This is not the life I would have ever imagined, but it's a terrific one. We don't get to choose our cards in life. All we can do is the best job we can with the cards that we're dealt.

Chapter 2

The Whats and Wheres of Allergens: Exposing Hidden and Harmful Ingredients

By need or choice, you are now eliminating the major allergens from your life. Your goal: To make allergy-friendly, delicious cookies for you and your family. But where to start? Let's start with a basic breakdown of information. I give a general description called the basics, which simply breaks down the common definition or function of each allergen; I discuss what the purpose the ingredient has in baking, I show the obvious and hidden sources of hidden allergens in ingredients, and some technical names you might find listed in packaged goods.

Although the "no" list may seem long, and you might feel overwhelmed, keep in mind that there is a long list of ingredients you *can* use! Remember, being prepared and aware keeps you and your family healthy and happy! For information on a general list of foods and products you should avoid, please refer to the "Helpful Websites" list on page 225. It's smart to ask a lot of questions before taking your first bite, especially if the food on your plate is a common allergen source. This list may not be all-inclusive. Make sure to do your own research and ask questions if you are unsure!

Gluten and Wheat

The basics: Gluten is a composite of the proteins gliadin and glutenin. Gliadin and glutenin comprise about 80 percent of the protein contained in wheat seed. These proteins are essential, giving bread the ability to rise properly and hold its shape in cooking. The gluten protein commonly found in wheat (durum, semolina, kamut, and spelt), rye, triticale, and barley literally acts like "glue" in your baked goods. Gluten is found in most mainstream bakeries, eateries, and prepared foods (like breads, pastas, crackers, and yes—cookies!).

It's important to remember that "wheat-free" does not necessarily mean "gluten-free," since the food might contain rye or barley. Wheat is one of the eight most common allergens in the United States and is, therefore, required to be listed on all food labels per FALCPA; gluten is not covered by FALCPA, however, and the FDA is developing a standard definition for gluten-free. Many brands now use the "wheat-free" logo on their packaging, but when you research the ingredients you might find that they are either contaminated through packaging or include barley or other gluten-containing grains. Your best bet is to stick with products that have the certified gluten-free emblem on them.

Purpose of gluten/wheat in baking: Wheat flour provides bulk and structure to baked goods. Gluten is the elasticity protein that traps carbon dioxide in the dough when combined with other ingredients to enable it to rise and to give your baked goods the feathery, soft, and chewy texture that dissolves in your mouth. Gluten helps your muffins develop, your pastry dough bind together, and your cookies keep their shape.

Obvious gluten sources: Flour, wheat flour, bleached white flour, whole grains, cereals, baking mixes, prepared refrigerated cookie dough, cookies, bran, hydrolyzed wheat protein, cake flour, pastry flour.

Hidden gluten sources: Baby food, candy and candy bars, malted foods (milk, candy, and powdered drinks), many brands of oats (although there are some gluten-free oats available), brewer's yeast, edible starch, farina, graham flour, kasha mix, sprouted grains, artificial colors, other coloring agents, dextrins, flavorings, glucose syrup, spice blends (may contain a thickener like flour or wheat starch), maltodextrin, maltose, soy sauce, natural flavoring.

Technical names you should also watch out for: Abyssinian hard wheat (Triticum-durum), Cereal binding, Triticum aestivum subspecies compactum, Dextrimaltose , Disodium wheatgermamido peg-2 sulfosuccinate, Durum wheat, (Triticum durum), Einkorn (Triticum monococcum), Emmer (Triticum dicoccon), Filler, Hydrolyzed wheat protein pg-propyl silanetriol, Hydrolyzed wheat starch, Hydroxypropyltrimonium hydrolyzed wheat protein,

Macha wheat (Triticum aestivum), Oriental wheat (Triticum turanicum), Pearl barley, Persian wheat (Triticum carthlicum), Poulard wheat (Triticum turgidum), Polish wheat (Triticum polonicum), Rice malt (if barley or Koji are used), Semolina triticum, Shot wheat (Triticum aestivum), Stearyldimoniumhydroxypropyl hydrolyzed wheat protein , Textured vegetable protein (TVP), Timopheevi wheat (Triticum timopheevii), Triticale X triticosecale, Vavilovi wheat (Triticum aestivum), Vegetable starch, Wheat, Abyssinian hard triticum durum, Wheat amino acids, Wheat durum triticum , Wheat germ glycerides, Wheat germamidopropyldimonium hydroxypropyl hydrolyzed wheat protein, Wheat triticum aestivum, Wheat triticum monococcum, Wheat (triticum vulgare) bran extract.

Dairy and Casein

The basics: Includes milk-based products (cream, butter, milk, casein, cheese, whey, yogurt, kefir, milk powders, condensed milk, etc.), derivatives and processes, from dairy cattle and dairy goat.

Casein is the protein that is found in animal milk, while lactose is the sugar. Many parents of autistic children report seeing behavioral and sensory improvements when gluten and casein are eliminated from their child's diet (GFCF diet). While there is limited scientific evidence to date, anecdotal evidence from many parents points to the benefits that may be gained from following a GFCF diet. For helpful resources on autism and the GFCF diet, see Chapter 9 of this book on page 223.

The main symptoms of dairy allergy or intolerance are gastrointestinal, dermatological, and respiratory. The symptoms may occur within a few minutes after exposure in immediate reactions, or after hours (and, in some cases, after several days) in delayed reactions. A true milk allergy is different than lactose/milk protein intolerance. For example,

- Milk allergy is a food allergy, an adverse immune reaction to a food protein that is normally harmless to the non-allergic individual.
- Lactose intolerance is a non-allergic food hypersensitivity that comes from a lack of production of the enzyme lactase, required to digest the predominant sugar in milk.
- Lactose intolerance is not actually a disease or malady, yet lactose maldigestion and intolerance affects more than 80 percent of the adult population of the world. It takes a much larger amount of milk to trigger adverse effects of lactose intolerance compared with milk allergy.

The kernels of grains (such as oat, corn, and rice) consist of three major parts:

Bran—the outer layer of the grain (14-16 percent of wheat, 5-6 percent of corn)
Endosperm—the main part of the grain
Germ—the smallest part of the grain.

Whole grains contain all three layers of the grain.

- Milk protein intolerance (MPI) is delayed reaction to a food protein that is normally harmless to the non-allergic, non-intolerant individual. Milk protein intolerance produces a non-IgE antibody and is not detected by allergy blood tests.
- MPI produces a range of symptoms very similar to milk allergy symptoms but can also include blood and/or mucus in the stool. Treatment for milk protein intolerance is the same as for milk allergy. Milk protein intolerance is also referred to as milk soy protein intolerance (MSPI).
- Casein accounts for nearly 80 percent of proteins in milk and cheese. In addition to being consumed in milk, casein is used in the manufacture of adhesives, binders, protective coatings, plastics (such as for knife handles and knitting needles), fabrics, food additives, and many other products. Casein has a molecular structure that is quite similar to that of gluten. Many gluten-free diets are combined with casein-free diets and referred to as a gluten-free, casein-free (GFCF) diet.

Purpose of dairy in baking: Butter consists of about 80 percent fat, 15 percent water, and 5 percent milk solids. Butter helps to tenderize and soften the texture of baked goods (which is especially helpful with gluten-free flours), it adds moistness and richness, assists in leavening, yields good melting qualities, helps to hold the shape of dough, and gives a delicious flavor. Higher fat–content dairy, including cream, sour cream, yogurt, and buttermilk, contributes texture, flavor, and color to dough and helps with leavening.

Obvious dairy sources: Milk, cream, butter, cheese, yogurt, buttermilk, nougat, puddings, milk chocolate and candies, frostings.

Hidden dairy sources: Artificial butter flavor, mayonnaise, margarine, baby food, chocolate, butter sprays, dairy-free substitutes (rice cheese, rice cream cheese), nondairy whipped topping, "natural ingredients."

Technical names you should also watch out for: Calcium caseinate, calcium sodium caseinate, potassium caseinate, sodium caseinate, acid casein, lactic acid casein, lactic casein, mineral acid casein, hydrolyzed casein, lactalbumin, whey protein lactalbumin, and other names that begin with lact.

Peanut

The basics: The peanut, or groundnut, is a species in the legume family. Edible peanuts account for two-thirds of the total peanut use in the United States. Early exposure can actually cause the beginning of a food allergy. After checking the ingredients list, look on the label for phrases like these: "May contain nuts," "Produced on shared equipment with nuts or peanuts," and "Produced in a facility that also processes nuts."

Cross contamination occurs when a safe food comes in contact with a food allergen such as peanut, tree nuts, seafood, or milk. For those with severe food allergies, eating even the slightest trace of an allergenic food can cause a potentially life threatening or fatal reaction. Although not everyone with a food allergy is this sensitive, it's still important to be very careful and follow precautions. Reactions can occur by several means:

- Eating a peanut
- Unknowingly eating a food that had been contaminated through an unintended ingredient or from being in contact with the peanut during preparation, storage, or serving.
- Touching something with peanut and then putting the hands in the mouth or touching the eyes. The most common instance of direct contact is when someone eats a peanut or nut product and then touches a chair or table, leaving even a trace of it. That residue could be enough to cause a reaction in the next person to use that table or chair.
- During food manufacturing through shared production and packaging equipment.
- Shared equipment (e.g., cheese and deli meats sliced on the same slicer) and through bulk display of food products (e.g., bins of baked goods, bulk nuts, etc.).
- During food preparation at restaurants through equipment, utensils, and hands.

Purpose of peanut in baking: Peanuts add crunch and flavor to baked goods. Peanut butter is high in fat and adds flavor, soft texture, and structure.

Obvious peanut sources: Peanuts, peanut oil, peanut flour, peanut starch, peanut brittle, candies, chocolates, peanut butter, marzipan, nougat, cakes, doughnuts, honey roasted peanuts, nut blends, Valencias (a European peanut brand).

Hidden peanut sources: Cereal, trail mix, food from bins at grocery stores, mandelonas, Nu-Nuts, ground nuts, flavorings, goober peas, icing, ice cream, granola, sulfite-free dried fruit, popcorn, gianduja, vegetarian products, plant proteins, oils.

Technical names you should also watch out for: Arachis and arachis oil, hydrogenated vegetable oils (if manufactured in a plant that produces peanut products).

TIP

Food Allergies at School
The Food Allergy and Anaphylaxis Network has put together guidelines for managing food allergies at schools and camps. They also provide a Food Allergy Action Plan you can fill out and submit to your child's school or camp for them to have on record. You can read them at www.foodallergy.org/school/guidelines.html.

Tree Nuts and Sesame

The basics: Tree nut allergy is slightly different than peanut allergy in that the types of nuts that cause the allergic reactions are not the same. Peanuts are considered legumes, whereas tree nuts are considered dry fruits. The symptoms of peanut allergy and tree nut allergy are the same, but a person with peanut allergies may not necessarily also be allergic to tree nuts, and vice versa. Tree nut allergies occur mainly, but not exclusively, in children. They are usually treated with an exclusion diet and vigilant avoidance of foods that may be contaminated with tree nuts or tree nut particles and/or oils.

Tree nuts include macadamia nuts, Brazil nuts, cashews, almonds, walnuts, pecans, pistachios, chestnuts, beechnuts, hazelnuts, pine nuts (pignoli or pinon), gingko nuts, shea, and hickory nuts. Coconut, the seed of a drupaceous fruit, has typically not been restricted in the diets of people with tree nut allergy. In October 2006, however, the FDA began identifying coconut as a tree nut. Nutmeg is obtained from the seeds of the tropical tree species; it is safe for an individual with a tree nut allergy, but always check with your doctor. The cashew is in the cashew botanical family along with mango and pistachio. An almond is actually in the plum family along with apricot, cherry, nectarine, peach, plum, and the prune plum, yet it is considered a tree nut by most allergists. It is possible to be allergic to almonds, yet be able to tolerate peaches or the other foods in the botanical family. The nuts of the shea tree yield a vegetable fat known as shea butter; they are considered nuts.

Sesame allergy is among the more common allergies in countries such as Israel and Australia where consumption of sesame-containing foods (like tahini paste) is high, and it's considered one of the ten major allergens by Health Canada. Check with your doctor to see if you should avoid these seeds as well.

Many people with peanut or tree nut allergies can safely tolerate sunflower seeds; however, we always recommend that you check with your doctor or allergist before eating them. You'll notice that several of the recipes in this cookbook call for sunflower seeds or sunflower seed butter. Several Enjoy Life products also include sunflower seeds, butter, or oil.

Purpose of tree nuts in baking: Tree nuts add flavor and crunch to a variety of baked goods. Nut oils and nut pastes are very popular to use in baking to add exotic flavor and texture.

Obvious tree nut sources: Trail mix, nut butters, cereals, ice cream, granola, sulfite-free dried fruit, oils, coconut milk.

Hidden tree nut sources: Baked goods, cookies, packaged foods.

Eggs

The basics: Egg allergies are one of the most common allergies of childhood. Both the yolk and the white of eggs are made of numerous proteins and are therefore potentially allergenic, although egg whites cause more reactions than yolks. Most egg allergies begin in childhood, but in rare cases egg allergies develop at older ages. As many as two-thirds of the children who are allergic to eggs outgrow their egg allergies by the age of seven.

People with allergies to hen's eggs may cross-react to two classes of foods: types of eggs (like duck and quail eggs), and poultry, especially chicken. While most people who are sensitive to eggs can eat chicken, there is one protein that is present in both eggs and poultry—alpha-livetin, or chicken serum albumin—that can cause allergies to both foods.

Flu vaccines are cultured in chicken eggs. Therefore, there is a potential for reaction in egg-allergic patients who receive the influenza vaccine.

Purpose of eggs in baking: Adds fat and protein, gives structure, produces a smooth batter, and contributes to volume and texture. Beaten eggs incorporate air in tiny cells or bubbles in the batter; this trapped air expands when heated and aids in leavening. Adds moisture, color, and rich flavor.

Obvious egg sources: Eggs in all forms (whites, yolks, whole eggs), puddings, custards, flan, baked goods, meringues.

Hidden egg sources: Packaged foods, candies, frostings, glazes.

Technical names you should also watch out for: Albumin, globulin, livetin, lysozyme, ovalbumin, ovoglobulin, ovomucin, ovomucoid, ovotransferrin, ovovitella, ovovitellin, silici albuminate, Simplesse, and vitellin.

Soy

The basics: Soy is often recommended to people who have allergies to gluten and dairy. Soy is very controversial in the medical field. Even people who are not allergic to soy should still research the pros and cons to this little bean. For people who are allergic, soy, like the other major allergens, is used in such a wide variety of baking products that you have to look out for cross contamination.

Purpose of soy in baking: Tofu is used as a replacement for dairy in puddings, pie fillings, and can replace fats like sour cream and eggs in baked goods. Margarines contain soy or soy proteins, which can replace butter by helping to bond the ingredients. Soy beverages add flavor and moisture to baked goods.

TIP

Aside from the obvious cookie ingredients (wheat in the flour, eggs in the dough, peanuts in the peanut butter, and soy in the margarine) many allergens hide in common ingredients and products that you may not suspect.

TIP

National Institutes of Allergy and Infectious Diseases Announces Grants to Stimulate Food Allergy Research

Twelve investigators have received grants to lead high-impact, innovative studies of food allergy. This program, called Exploratory Investigations in Food Allergy, is funded by the National Institute of Allergy and Infectious Diseases (NIAID), part of the National Institutes of Health, and two advocacy groups, the Food Allergy and Anaphylaxis Network (FAAN) and the Food Allergy Project (FAP). The initiative will support research on the factors that contribute to the development of food allergy, the relationship between other immune system disorders and food allergy, and the epidemiology and genetics of food allergy. An additional goal is to encourage investigators who have not previously been funded for studies of food allergy to move into the field. You can learn more at www.nih.gov/news/health/jun2008/niaid-30.htm.

Obvious soy sources: Edamame, soy fiber, soy flour, soy grits, soy milk, soy nuts, soy sprouts, Soya, soybean curd, soy butter, margarine, alternative nut butters, tofu.

Hidden soy sources: Protein concentrate/isolate, flavorings, vegetable gum, soy lecithin, starch, multigrains, doughnuts, doughnut mix, pancake mix, flour blends, smoothies, cream sauces and packets, gluten-free and dairy-free packaged foods and baking ingredients, shortening, cooking oils, mass-produced chocolate products.

Technical names you should also watch out for: Albumin, textured vegetable protein (TVP), hydrolyzed vegetable protein (HVP), natural and artificial flavorings, vegetable gum and starch.

Sulfites

The basics: Sulfites are compounds that contain the sulfite ion and can be a source of food allergies/intolerances. Sulfites are considered one of the ten most common allergens in Canada, and the US FDA requires food manufacturers and processors to disclose the presence of sulfating agents in concentrations of at least 10 parts per million (PPM), but the threshold may be even lower. They are often used as preservatives in dried fruits, dried potatoes, and wine to prevent spoilage and oxidation. Look for sulfite-free dried fruits if you suspect that you are sulfite-allergic or sensitive.

Purpose of sulfites in baking: Acts as a preservative in many packaged foods like fruits, nuts, and flavorings.

Obvious sulfite sources: Grapes, fruit (canned, fresh, juice, or dried), coconut, cereal, trail mix, syrups (corn, maple, pancake), granola, canned fruit pie filling, ciders, fruit juice, fresh vegetables, most condiments, dried fruits.

Hidden sulfite sources: Beet sugars, glazed fruits, frosting, baby formulas, baby food, cornmeal, bottled lemon and lime juice, gelatin, hard candy, textured vegetable protein, unsulfured molasses.

Technical names you should also watch out for: Sodium sulfite, sodium bisulfite, sodium metabisulfite, potassium bisulfite, potassium metabisulfite, sulfur dioxide, anything ending in "sulfite."

Shellfish/Fish

The basics: Even though this is a cookie cookbook and we usually don't use fish and shellfish in our sweets, it is important to address where these allergens can hide. Allergies to seafood include both fish and shellfish. Seafood (finned fish like tuna, cod, and salmon) and shellfish (shrimp, crab, lobster, scallops, squid) can cause an overreaction of the immune system, which may lead to severe physical symptoms for millions of people. The Asthma and Allergy Foundation of America estimates that the majority of pediatric and adult food allergy patients have a seafood allergy. It occurs mainly, but not exclusively, in children. While fish and shellfish are not related foods, these foods are usually found in the same place (restaurants). Reactions to seafood can be severe and potentially life-threatening. Allergy to either of these foods is less likely to be outgrown, and therefore is commonly seen in adults. The allergic compounds in seafood can be conducted through the air when it is being cooked or when people around you are eating fish.

Obvious fish sources: Oils, fried foods (cooked in same oil as fish), fish, shellfish, fish sticks, fish products, sushi, imitation crab, omega-3 supplements, oyster sauce and other Asian sauces, and Worcestershire sauce.

Chapter 3

Stocking an Allergy-Friendly Kitchen

You know what you can't eat, and now you are ready
to make some cookies with allergy-friendly ingredients
that you *can* eat! Let's stock up our kitchens with
ingredients that we can use to make all of these
yummy cookies!

TIP

Your doctor/allergist and you are the ones who need to choose which ingredients and products will work best for you and your family. In most ingredients, there is a contamination risk. Research the product and consult your physician to make sure the product works for you. If your allergies are severe and you react to the tiniest amount of contamination, some of the products that I use may not work for you. For example, certain flours I recommend are made in a facility that also processes nuts, soy, and dairy. That may not bother many people, but for some it can cause a reaction. Always check with the company frequently because their facilities can change.

Where to find this stuff!

After each section of baking needs there is a "Find It" segment with information on where to get the items you need.

Flours and starches

There are currently many gluten-free flours on the market. Since we are also avoiding peanuts and tree nuts, potato, and soy, we are a little more limited in our choices. But that is ok! Luckily, the flours I use in these recipes are available at many grocery stores or online.

Rice flour: Bob's Red Mill® white rice flour works best for taste, and the brown rice flour adds a bit of nutrients. Regular rice flour is a fine, powdery flour made from regular white rice. It's used mainly for baked goods and is a staple in gluten-free baking. Rice flour might leave a gritty texture, but it always allows the true flavor of your baked goods to come through.

Tapioca flour: A starchy substance extracted from the root of the cassava plant, the flour is used as a thickening agent for soups, fruit fillings, glazes, and baking. Also mix it with rice flour and use this flour combination to replace the function of the wheat flour and eggs. Tapioca flour is different from tapioca starch or arrowroot starch; do not confuse the two. If a recipe calls for tapioca starch or arrowroot starch, do not use tapioca flour.

Tapioca starch: I do call on tapioca starch or arrowroot starch, instead of the flour, in a few recipes. The starch is a key ingredient in recipes like the shortbread cookies. You can find tapioca starch or arrowroot starch in Asian markets or natural food stores. I would be careful purchasing starch from sources that are not made in the United States due to contamination risks. If you cannot find tapioca starch and are allergic to cornstarch, try using arrowroot starch. If you choose to use tapioca flour instead of starch, your product might be more gelatinous; the flavor will still be good though. It is your choice.

Arrowroot starch: Arrowroot starch is used as a thickener. If you cannot use or find tapioca starch or cornstarch, replace with this starch.

Flax meal: Ground flaxseeds make this hearty and nutritious flour, which is high in fiber and omega-3s. It does go rancid quickly, so it needs to be refrigerated. My best advice is to buy in small packages and keep in the refrigerator.

Certified gluten-free rolled oats and oat flour: Oats are somewhat controversial for people with Celiac Disease. Please refer to the Wheat and Gluten section in Chapter 2. To make oat bran or oat flour, which is called for in a few recipes, you may purchase certified gluten-free rolled oats (such as the brands Cream Hill Estates, Gifts of Nature, and PrOatino) and place them in a non-contaminated coffee grinder or food processor. Grind into a fine flour (the finer the better for oat flour; for oat bran, just grind until you have a coarse consistency). You may also go to your favorite online allergy-friendly vendor to purchase oats and oat flour. Just make sure the contamination risks are suitable for your family's needs. Oat flour provides nutrients, fiber, and a whole grain flavor. It works wonders in gluten-free baking because it contains starches that help your product bind together. If you cannot use oats of any kind, you may substitute rolled rice, quinoa flakes, or buckwheat flakes for certified gluten-free rolled oats.

Rice bran: A highly nutritious food with a pleasant nutty flavor. It is a good source of dietary fiber (25 percent of your daily recommended allowance) and is mostly insoluble. Rice bran is the outer coating of the rice kernel. It's great to use in baking to add nutrients, flavor, and texture. Rice bran can go rancid quickly, so you may want to keep it in the refrigerator.

Cornmeal and flour: Many people have to avoid corn, so I do not call for corn flour in the book. You may replace corn flour with millet flour in other recipes if desired.

Sorghum: A millet-like grain, sorghum is America's third leading cereal crop. It is a powerhouse of nutrition and adds a superb whole-wheat flavor to gluten-free baking. Use in a flour mix for best results. Sorghum is also known as milo and grest millet. It adds great taste and nutrition to recipes and baked goods, and it's also high in insoluble fiber.

Millet: Millet flour has a subtle flavor, lots of vitamins and minerals, and adds a lovely creamy color to baked goods. Mix with other grains when baking for best results. You can substitute it for cornmeal or corn flour.

Quinoa flour: Quinoa (pronounced keen-wa) is the most nutritious grain available. It is also one of the oldest cultivated grains in the world. Quinoa is high in protein, calcium, and iron. Use this delicate flour when baking with a mixture of other grains. Quinoa also comes in flakes and can be used in place of certified gluten-free rolled oats.

Buckwheat flour and flakes: Buckwheat is high in nutrients. My kids do not like the bold flavor of this grain in products like cookies. Some recipes with lots of spices could tolerate this flour. You may replace rice bran, sorghum, or flax for buckwheat in the recipes, or vice versa, if you like. Buckwheat flakes also make a good gluten-free substitution for oat flakes, if desired.

Rolled rice flakes: Rice flakes are roasted and pressed into flakes on stainless steel rollers. Many brands are whole grain, which makes them higher in nutrients. Rice flakes are a great alternative to certified gluten-free rolled oats.

Teff flour: A uniquely flavored whole-grain flour. It adds an appealing taste and good nutrition to your baked goods. I use this flour in my hearty crust recipes.

Are oats safe to eat on a gluten-free diet?

In the past, people with Celiac Disease have generally avoided oats; however, there are now several certified gluten-free oat brands available, such as Cream Hill Estates, Gifts of Nature, and PrOatino. If you have Celiac Disease, you should talk with your doctor and do your own research on oats, since each person's health concerns are different. You'll notice that we've included oats in some of the recipes in this cookbook, but if you're not comfortable eating them, quinoa or rice flakes work really well too! Most oats can become contaminated with wheat during transport and processing. Oats are a great product to use in allergy-free cooking, but you and your doctor have to make the best call for your family.

FIND IT

Bob's Red Mill® (www.bobsredmill.com)

Bob's Red Mill company produces an extensive line of certified organic and gluten-free baking products, flours, and mixes. Please contact the company regarding contamination for other allergens. Here is a quote from their website, as of 2008, about their gluten-free symbol (on all their gluten-free flours and mixes): "We segregate our ingredients and thoroughly clean our equipment between production lines. This symbol also informs consumers that while there is no recognized standard, we only place our gluten-free symbol on those products that meet our standard of no more than 20 parts per million, which we establish through a gluten test performed in our quality control laboratory. Each product is tested before milling and after packaging. In an effort to better serve our allergen-sensitive consumers, our gluten-free facility is also dairy- and casein-free."

They offer: Arrowroot starch, baking powder, baking soda, buckwheat flour and flakes, corn flour, cornmeal, cornstarch, flax meal, millet flour, quinoa flour, rice bran, white and brown rice flour, sorghum flour, xanthan gum, and more. Products found in most grocery stores and online.

FLOUR BLENDS

Everyone has their own taste preferences, so I want to give a few choices for your enjoyment! I have made and purchased several flours and blends that are gluten-, soy-, potato-, egg-, and tree nut-free. In my family, we prefer taste over texture. We find that many blends may be a bit (not significantly) less gritty than others, but the downside is that they often leave a bitter aftertaste, or you are replacing the gritty texture for a powdery texture. Many people whose children are very picky and are not eating a variety of nutritious foods may want to use more nutritious flours instead of my rice and tapioca primary blends. You may play with a mix of flours; for example, potato flour and starch (if not an allergy) adds a soft texture and nice taste. Millet, quinoa, buckwheat, and sorghum are all flours that provide good nutrients. Although I prefer the taste of white rice flour and tapioca flours, if you simply want more nutrients or do not like the slightly gritty texture of rice flour, try the flour mix on the facing page.

Mock Whole Wheat Flour Blend

1 ½ cups (185 g) Bob's Red Mill
   tapioca flour
1 cup (130 g) cornstarch or
   (100 g) rice bran

½ cup (60 g) fava flour (if you can
   tolerate bean flours) or flaxmeal
1 ½ cups (185 g) sorghum flour
1 teaspoon (3 g) xanthan gum
   (optional)

DIRECTIONS

- In a large bowl combine all ingredients and mix well with a whisk. Store in a 6-cup (1.4 L) glass container with a lid. If you use rice bran, store in the refrigerator. Otherwise, you may store in a dark, cool place like the pantry or a cupboard.

- How to use: Use this blend in place of the rice flour and tapioca flour combination I call for in many of the recipes. For example, a recipe will say 1 cup (125 g) rice flour and ½ cup (65 g) tapioca starch or arrowroot starch. Instead, use 1½ cups (185 g) Mock Whole Wheat Flour Blend. Some recipes call for flax meal, certified gluten-free rolled oats or rice flakes, or additional rice bran; *do not* replace for those ingredients. Only use this blend to substitute for the combined amount of rice flour and tapioca flour.

RECIPE NOTE

Note that replacing the flour will change the outcome of the recipe a bit.
I indicate if a recipe should not be modified.

Butter and Egg Substitutes

Currently there are no margarines that are free of the combination of dairy, nuts, casein, soy, and/or gluten. Certain medical research suggests that "highly refined oils" do not contain the protein (such as soy or nut) that causes the allergic reactions. Call the manufacturing company and always check with your doctor/allergist to make sure that these oils are safe for you to use. I do not use margarines because in my recipes I want to deliver the best sure bet for families with allergies. Instead, I use the following products.

Spectrum Organic Shortening: Nominal melting point is 96.8 to100.4°F (36 to 38°C). This shortening is approximately 50 percent saturated and 50 percent unsaturated fat and contains no transisomerized fats, which are found in hydrogenated oils. Spectrum uses palm fruit oil (PFO) from the spineless palm tree (*Elaesis guineensis*) in its shortening, which contains no trans fat. Spectrum Organic Shortening works as a good base in many cookies. At its processing plant, Spectrum makes a variety of oils that include nuts and soy. For additional information, contact their customer service department at 1-800-343-7833.

You may use your favorite safe shortening but please note that all of my recipes were designed using this brand of shortening and use of a different product may yield different results.

Expeller-pressed vegetable oil: I prefer to use canola, olive, and safflower oil in my recipes. You have to decide what works best for you. Do note that many vegetable oil blends contain soy.

Egg replacer: Usually in powder form, egg replacer mimics what eggs do in recipes and greatly simplifies baking for people who cannot use eggs. It replaces egg whites as well as egg yolks in baking. It may contain potato flour, so I do not use it in this cookbook.

Unsweetened applesauce: Purchase organic unsweetened applesauce with no added sugar or flavoring. Unsweetened applesauce can replace eggs and fats in your baked goods. In this book, I usually combine the unsweetened applesauce with fats, like oils or Spectrum Organic Shortening, to give the cookie a softer texture. If you happen to be allergic to apples, replace the amount of unsweetened applesauce with puréed pears, yellow squash, bananas, or prunes. It will change the flavor, but if you need a substitution, give it a try.

FIND IT

You should be able to find these items, like oils and unsweetened applesauce, at your local grocery stores, natural food stores, and Whole Foods Market. Look for organic brands. A reminder! If your grocery store does not carry an item, talk to the manager.

General Substitutions for Egg- and Dairy-Free Baking

Instead of calling for a pre-made egg replacement mixture throughout the book, I list everything you need for each recipe. Each cookie recipe has a different chemistry and requires a variety of formulas for flour, butter, and egg substitutions.

As a general substitution for egg- and dairy-free baking in other recipes, cream together ¼ cup (50 g) Spectrum Organic Shortening, ¼ cup (60 ml) vegetable oil, and ¼ cup (60 ml) water, and ¼ teaspoon (1.5 g) salt with the sugar in your recipe. This is a good substitute for ¼ cup (55 g) of butter.

If you are looking for potato- and corn-free egg replacer, choose from one of the following: 1 tablespoon (7 g) flax meal, ¼ teaspoon (1.2 g) baking powder, and a dash of salt (equivalent to one egg) OR 2 teaspoons (2.5 g) Bob's Red Mill tapioca flour, ½ teaspoon (2.3 g) baking powder, and a dash of salt (equivalent to one egg).

If you are not comfortable using Spectrum Organic Shortening or oils of any kind due to possible contamination, you can replace the amount of oil or shortening with half unsweetened applesauce and half water. Example, if a recipe calls for ½ cup (120 ml) oil or (100 g) Spectrum Organic Shortening, replace with ¼ cup (60 g) unsweetened applesauce and (60 ml) ¼ cup water. Do this even if the recipe calls for water and unsweetened applesauce already. The cookie will seem a bit drier (and in fruit recipes, like pumpkin bars, will appear wetter), and it will not spread like some cookies do, but the flavor will still be good. If you are trying to avoid shortening, choose the frostings, like glazes, that do not have shortening in them.

Vanilla beans come from a
tropical orchid that bears
the only edible fruit of the
orchid family, the largest
family of flowering plants in
the world. Although there
are about 150 varieties of
vanilla extract, only two
orchid species produce
commercially viable vanilla
beans: Planifolia (Bourbon)
and Tahitian.

Baking Necessities

Baking powder: A mixture of baking soda and an acid (like cream of tartar). I use double-acting baking powder in my recipes.

Baking soda: Otherwise known as sodium bicarbonate. When moisture and acid (like packed brown sugar or unsulfured molasses) are present, the soda releases carbon dioxide gas, which leavens the product.

Cream of tartar: Best known for helping stabilize and give more volume to beaten egg whites. It is the acidic ingredient in some brands of baking powder. It is also used to produce a creamier texture in sugary desserts such as candy and frosting.

Extracts: I use liquid vanilla extract because it works best with the dough. If you prefer powdered vanilla extract, equal amounts of water. For example, if the recipe calls for 1 teaspoon (5 ml) vanilla extract, use 1 teaspoon (5 g) powdered vanilla and 1 teaspoon (5 ml) water. Most vanilla extracts are gluten-free, but call the manufacturing company to be sure. Some are made with corn alcohol, although many venders say that all corn protein is removed in the distillation process. Check with your doctor about proteins and distillation before consuming. I do use peppermint extract; check with manufacturing companies to make sure it is safe for you.

Salt: Butter, margarine, and eggs have naturally occurring sodium in them, but we do not use those ingredients in these cookies and instead add a small amount of salt to the recipes. I find that salt plays a huge role as a flavor enhancer in these baked goods. If you do not want to add salt to your treat, you may omit the salt in the recipe.

Spices: Spices add yumminess! In this book we call on ground cinnamon, ginger, nutmeg, and cloves to zest up some cookies. You can make your own pumpkin pie spice by combining 1½ teaspoons (3.5 g) ground cinnamon, 1 teaspoon (1.8 g) ground ginger, ¼ teaspoon (0.6 g) ground nutmeg, and ⅛ teaspoon (0.3 g) ground cloves. If a recipe calls for 1 teaspoon (1.7 g) of pumpkin pie spice, measure out 1 teaspoon (1.7 g) from this mixture.

Unsweetened cocoa powder: There are a few cocoa powders to choose from, so you'll have to research manufacturing companies to find the brand that works best for your allergies. I use a cocoa powder that is not alkalized.

FIND IT

Your local grocery store, natural food stores, and places like Whole Foods Market are good spots to pick up these items. Bob's Red Mill and Ener-G Foods offer varieties of baking needs like baking powder and soda and can be found in stores or ordered online.

Try to buy pure vanilla extract like Nielsen-Massey Vanilla Extract (certified gluten-free but does contain corn alcohol) or Cook's Cookbook Alcohol-Free Pure Vanilla Extract (gluten- and corn alcohol–free).

Purchase small quantities of organic spices for fresher taste and purity. There are many you can choose from, and you can find them at natural food stores, Whole Foods Markets, and grocery stores. Do not purchase spices from a bin type of container; instead, buy sealed bottles.

Sugars

Brown sugar: Brown sugar is manufactured by adding molasses back to refined sugar. There are two grades—light and dark—with the dark containing more molasses.

Granulated sugar: Also called table sugar. Adds sweetness and flavor, tenderizes, gives crust color, increases keeping qualities by retaining moisture, and acts as a creaming agent with fats.

Honey: Varies in flavor and color depending on the source. Honey contains invert sugars and helps retain moisture in baked goods. It also provides flavor.

Powdered sugar: Often called confectionary sugar, purchased powdered sugar contains cornstarch. To make corn-free powdered sugar, see the sidebar.

Raw sugar: Demerara or turbinado sugar (often sold as Sugar in the Raw®) is simply natural sugar crystals that haven't been bleached or over-processed. It is the result of slow boiling a layer of highly colored cane sugar, allowing the crystals to retain their natural unsulfured molasses. Using it in baking adds crunch. I generally bake with it as a topping on the cookies.

Superfine sugar: Finer than regular granulated sugar. In baking it makes a more uniform batter and can support higher quantities of fat. I call for superfine sugar in the majority of my recipes because I like the way it performs with the taste and structure of the baked goods.

Unsulfured molasses: Concentrated sugar cane juice. Unsulfured molasses is a byproduct of sugar refining. It is what remains after most of the sugar has been extracted from cane juice. Sulfured molasses is not a byproduct but is a specially manufactured sugar product that contains sulfur dioxide as a preservative. It has a more bitter taste than unsulfured molasses. Darker grades are stronger in flavor and contain less sugar than lighter grades. Unsulfured molasses retains moisture in baked goods and helps to prolong freshness. I use organic unsulfured molasses.

FIND IT

These basic ingredients are available at your local grocery store and natural food stores. Look for organic when possible. Interestingly, when you cook allergy-friendly you do not have to add

Corn-Free Powdered Sugar Recipe

So far I have not been able to find a corn-free powdered sugar. But with the right tools, you can come pretty darn close to making it yourself. I have found the best results by using a non-contaminated large coffee grinder, ideally one that can hold 1 cup (200 g) or 1/2 cup (100 g) of sugar at a time. **The ratio is 1 tablespoon (8 g) tapioca or arrowroot starch to 1 cup (200 g) superfine sugar.** Unfortunately you have to make it in small batches. Grind until you have a very soft, fine powder—the finer the better. Pour into a large resealable plastic bag or sealed glass or stainless steel container. If you have a heavy-duty blender you can give that a try and make larger batches. Store in a cool dark place.

as much sugar as you would otherwise. Rice and tapioca flours tend to be sweeter flours. For example, in my chocolate chip cookies, ½ cup (115 g) of packed brown sugar is sufficient for sweetening, compared with 1 cup (200 g) granulated sugar plus 1 cup (225 g) packed brown sugar in most basic cookie doughs.

Other good stuff

Decorations: Candies, chocolates, sprinkles, and colored sugar. Go online to www.allerneeds.com to find candy products that are suitable for your allergy needs. Check with your doctor/allergist and the manufacturing company to make sure the product is safe. I rely on many Enjoy Life Foods products like chocolate chips, boom CHOCO boom bars, and Not Nuts! trail mixes for the topping and décor on many cookies. Raw sugar adds a nice touch sprinkled over frosted cookies. If food coloring is safe for you, add a few drops of food coloring to ½ cup (100 g) of raw sugar, stir well, and you have a safe variation of colored sugar to jazz up your cookies and cakes.

Lemon and lime juice and zest: Your best bet is to use fresh lemons and limes, especially if you have a sulfite allergy. For those who do not have this allergy, try to purchase pure organic bottled or frozen lemon concentrate with no added sulfites. I use Santa Cruz Organic® Lemon and Lime juices, which come in glass bottles.

Marshmallows: Mini and regular size. The marshmallows I have found either have corn or fish gelatin in them. A few recipes require the use of marshmallows for the base of the cookie, like in cereal bars. If you cannot have corn or fish, there are many other recipes for your enjoyment. In the recipes that call for you to add marshmallows, you can usually replace them with your favorite trail mix, chocolate chips, or dried fruit.

Pineapple: A few recipes call for pineapple, referring to canned pineapple. Fresh pineapple is too acidic and doesn't perform as well in the recipes. Look for pineapple in juice, not syrup. For best results, drain the juice from the can and lay the pineapple pieces (excluding crushed pineapple) on a paper towel to remove the excess liquid.

Pumpkin: I prefer to use organic canned pumpkin. Canned pumpkin is consistent, easy to use, and available year-round when I'm craving something pumpkin.

Seeds: Pumpkin seeds and sunflower seeds give our recipes a crunchy kick. Make sure you purchase seeds that are not contaminated with nuts and nut oils. You may use raw seeds or roasted and salted seeds in these recipes if you choose.

Other goodies: Sunflower butter (chunky or smooth), organic berries, bananas, rice milk, other alternative milk beverages, and many other simple items found throughout the book can easily be found in most large grocery stores, Whole Foods Markets, and natural food stores.

Enjoy Life products: Enjoy Life® Snickerdoodle soft baked cookies, Enjoy Life® Double Chocolate Brownie soft baked cookies, Enjoy Life® Lively Lemon soft baked cookies, Enjoy Life® Happy Apple™ soft baked cookies, Enjoy Life® semi-sweet chocolate chips, Enjoy Life® Cranapple Crunch granola, Enjoy Life® Very Berry Crunch granola, Enjoy Life® Cinnamon Crunch granola, Enjoy Life® Not Nuts!™ Mountain Mambo™ trail mix, Enjoy Life® Not Nuts!™ Beach Bash™ trail mix, Enjoy Life® boom CHOCO boom™ chocolate bars (dairy-free rice milk bar, dairy-free rice milk with crispy rice bar, dark chocolate bar), Enjoy Life® Perky O's cereal, Enjoy Life® Perky's™ "Nutty" Rice™, Enjoy Life® Perky's™ "Nutty" Flax™

FIND IT

You can find most of these products at large grocery stores, natural food stores, Whole Foods Markets, and online. For Enjoy Life products, check www.enjoylifefoods.com to find a store near you that carries the brand.

Chapter 4

Allergy-Friendly Baking 101

Having the right tools in the kitchen, understanding baking instructions, and storing your baked goods properly can make a big difference in improving your ability to make successful cookies. If you are new to baking or allergy-friendly baking, this chapter is very important to read.

Helpful Cookie-Making Tools

The first helpful tool is in your thinking! Always remember that positive thinking and a good attitude when cooking or serving allergy-friendly foods is the key. It's strategy, not stress!

When I began baking and creating I started out with the very basics in kitchen supplies and tools, and it took many years to build up the collection of all the great kitchen items I have today. My foods were just as good then as they are today, but some of the tools make things easier and less time consuming.

BASIC NEEDS

- 6- to 9-cup (1.4- to 2.1-L) glass containers with lids or metal sealable bins
- 8-inch (20-cm) square baking pan
- 9-inch (23-cm) square baking pan
- 9 x 13-inch (23 x 33-cm) rectangular baking pan
- Aluminum foil
- Box grater/Citrus zester
- Cookie cutters, in a variety of themes and sizes
- Cooling racks
- Electric mixer (It is imperative that you have a quality hand mixer or preferably a stationary mixer such as a Kitchen Aid. When baking with alternative foods, it is helpful to have the mixing and creaming abilities of an electric mixer that you just can't achieve mixing by hand.)
- Food processor
- Frying pan, small
- Heavy baking or cookie sheets (flat metal sheets with two or three rimless sides)
- Heavy duty resealable plastic bags
- High-powered blender or non-contaminated coffee grinder
- Ice cream or cookie scoop, in a variety of sizes
- Icing spatula (non–sharp, flat, flexible blade)
- Large metal spatula (with a thin, very flat tip)
- Liquid measuring cups, glass 1- or 2-cup (235- or 475-ml) sizes
- Dry measuring cups, metal or plastic in ¼, ⅓, ½, and 1 cup (57, 76, 115, and 230 g) sizes
- Measuring spoons, ¼ teaspoon (1.3 ml), ½ teaspoon (2.5 ml), 1 teaspoon (5 ml), and 1 tablespoon (15 ml)

- Mini muffin pan or mini tart pan
- Mixing bowls, in a variety of sizes
- Parchment paper
- Pizza pan, small or medium
- Plastic wrap
- Pot holders
- Powdered sugar sifter or a sieve
- Rolling pin
- Rubber spatula, in a variety of sizes
- Saucepans, in a variety of sizes
- Springform pan (round baking pan with removable sides)
- Wooden spoons

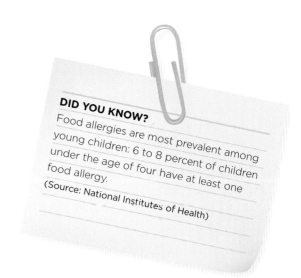

DID YOU KNOW?
Food allergies are most prevalent among young children: 6 to 8 percent of children under the age of four have at least one food allergy.
(Source: National Institutes of Health)

Pan variations: If you do not have a 9 x 13-inch (23 x 33-cm) pan, use two 8-inch (20-cm) square baking pans. Bake at the same temperature, but subtract about 5 to 7 minutes off the baking time. If you do not have a mini muffin tin, use a regular size muffin tin and increase baking time by about 10 minutes or until the baked good is done according to the recipe description (golden, firm in the middle, etc.).

HOW TO MEASURE
Just a reminder:

3 teaspoons = 1 tablespoon = 15 ml

2 tablespoons = 1 fluid ounce = 30 ml

4 tablespoons = ¼ cup = 60 ml

1 cup = 8 fluid ounces = 235 ml

Liquids (milk, water, oil): Use a glass measuring cup, place on a flat surface, and pour in the liquid to the exact line that is required. Check the line at eye level to make sure it is exact.

Dry ingredients (flour, starch, certified gluten-free rolled oats): Generously spoon ingredients into the proper size measuring cups. Take a flat spatula and level the ingredient by running the straight edge of the blade over the rim of the measuring cup. The surface of the ingredient should be even with the rim of the cup.

Shortening: Liberally fill a dry measuring cup with the shortening; with a spatula, level off the top as described for the dry ingredients.

A dash: In general, this measurement is used in reference to salt. A dash is 1 shake of salt or a spice with a shaker lid firmly on the container. Some people really like what salt does to flavor; if you are one of those bakers, by all means experiment with the amount of salt—you may like a dash, or two or three! For those who avoid sodium, omit the salt if needed.

Dry foods (trail mix, cereal, sulfite-free dried fruit, chocolate chips): Use dry measuring cups and pour the ingredient into the cup to the top, keeping it reasonably even with the lip of the measuring cup.

Directions to Recipes
WHAT DOES IT MEAN TO MIX?

Always use your best judgment when baking. Elevation, brands of ingredients, and the types of tools you use can affect the outcome of your product. For example, if the recipe states to cream for 1 minute until fluffy, and you have followed the directions but the batter is still watery, by all means—cream it a little longer until you achieve the correct consistency! I use descriptive words in the recipes (dough should be firm, soft, crumbly, etc.) to help you try to create the best results. Follow the directions, refer to the descriptive words, and use your best judgment. Don't worry! The recipes are truly easy; I just want to give you the basics!

Ingredients

The first step in each of these recipes is generally to mix or cream together the first few listed ingredients. Some recipes require you to "cream" together a few ingredients like you would do with sugar, eggs, and butter, but in allergy-friendly baking it does not necessarily mean only your wet ingredients. For example, the recipe may require your sugar, starch, and oil to be blended together before adding the flours to mimic the function of the conventional ingredients, like eggs, that we are not using. Some recipes require mixing flours with the oil to help create a creamy blend.

Remaining Ingredients

Generally, the second step to the recipe is adding the "remaining ingredients." It requires you to blend in ingredients like the flours and baking powder, commonly referred to in many cookbooks as the "dry" ingredients. You will add the "remaining ingredients" to the first set of ingredients that you have creamed or mixed together. Combine until you have a smooth dough; I pause to scrape down the bowl at this point to make sure that the ingredients have not stuck to the sides of the mixer or processor and to make sure that all the ingredients are blended together.

You do have the option of sifting the dry ingredients together if you choose, but it is optional—and time-consuming. It does incorporate the ingredients well and sometimes makes the baked good lighter. It is up to you. I have not sifted dry ingredients in making these cookies.

Add In and Stir In

This usually means to remove the dough from the mixer or food processer and stir in these ingredients by hand with a wooden spoon until they are evenly distributed throughout the dough. You may opt to leave ingredients in the mixer or processor if desired. In a mixer, just mix on low for a few seconds. In a processor, hit the pulse button a few times.

Creaming

Creaming is the process of beating fat and sugar together to incorporate air, which is important in making cookies. Start the mixer slowly to incorporate the ingredients indicated. With a spatula, scrape down the sides of the bowl. Remove the spatula and slowly turn the mixer on to medium or medium-high speed. Air will incorporate and the mixture should look as if it grew in size. This process should take about 45 seconds to 1 minute. The mixture should be smooth and creamy without lumps and almost have a glossy appearance. Some recipes might require more or less time, as indicated in the directions. At this stage you are ready to add the next set of ingredients.

Mix and Blend

When using an electric mixer, these two words basically mean the same thing: Incorporate the batter on medium speed until well combined. In a food processor, it generally means to pulse rapidly or turn the processor on for about 30 seconds or until the dough forms into a ball.

Stir

By hand, use a wooden spoon to stir the ingredients until smooth, or run the mixer on low for less than 6 seconds to combine dough.

Pulse

This applies when you use a food processor and is commonly used in this cookbook. Hit the pulse button several times to mix the dough.

Drizzle

In this cookbook, I sometimes suggest drizzling powdered sugar icing or melted chocolate over the cookies. You may use a spoon and generously pour in a thin stream over the cookies. I prefer putting the mixture (make sure it is not too hot) into a heavy-duty resealable plastic bag. Cut a tip off one of the corners of the bag and use like a pastry bag to decorate, drizzle, or make zigzags over cookies.

Greasing a Baking Pan

To grease a baking pan usually means to lightly spread butter or spray oil on the pan to help prevent sticking and help to make the edges of the baked good golden. Since we do not use butter, and I have not been able to find an oil spray that does not contain soy, my suggestion is to dampen a paper towel with vegetable oil and spread it around the pan, focusing on the sides, corners, and bottom. You may use this method with your mini muffin and tart pans as well.

Lining a Baking Pan

You may use aluminum foil or oven-safe or nonstick baking parchment paper. For a cookie sheet, line the bottom of the pan. For a cake pan, a great tip is to turn the pan over, face down, and form the foil or paper over the bottom of the pan. Lift the foil or paper off, and it will hold the shape of the baking pan. Flip the pan back over and place the formed foil or paper into the bottom of the pan. Some recipes require you to grease the lined baking pan/sheet. Follow the same directions for greasing a foil-lined pan as a regular pan.

Remove to a Flat Surface

When the directions require you to move the cookie to a flat surface, it generally means to use a flat spatula and carefully remove the cookie to a cooling rack. It has been my experience that flat surfaces like a glass plate or serving tray work better than a slotted cooling rack because delicate gluten-free cookies are often too breakable until they've completely cooled, and I find that I have more successful cookies when I lay them on a flat, even surface to cool.

Helpful Hints

YOUR OVEN

Ovens vary—some cook at high temperatures, and some are old and take forever to preheat. The lucky ones have a convection oven that bakes the cookies perfectly. Regardless of what you have to cook with, you need to know your oven's temperament. My oven is an older gas oven and bakes things quickly. Get to know your oven and pay attention to its baking speed.

When you decide to make some cookies, turn your oven on first thing. By the time you get your supplies together and your dough made, your oven should be at the correct temperature and ready to go! Some ovens might take up to 20 minutes to fully preheat. The rack positioning also can make a difference. I place mine in the middle of the oven.

If a recipe calls for the cookies to bake for 10 minutes or until golden brown around the edges, and your cookies are not browned after 10 minutes, keep baking and check them every 2 minutes until the cookie matches the description in the recipe.

I often give suggestions for how many cookies should be placed on the baking sheet for each recipe, but as a general rule, space your cookies out about 4 inches (10 cm) apart. On an average-size baking sheet, I usually place 6 cookies per sheet. My suggestion is to bake only 1 or 2 sheets at a time.

Some cookies can be golden on the outside and still be pretty soft on the inside. If the recipe states to take them out when they are golden but soft in the middle, do so. Cookies continue cooking on the baking sheet even after you take them out of the oven.

If you find that your cookies are burning on the bottoms, try doubling up your baking sheets with one sheet on top of another, or purchase a heavy-gauge pan or one with an air-cushion inset.

My family prefers softer cookies over crunchy cookies. You can adjust the baking time, a little more or less, to achieve your desired cookie product. Remember, more baking time yields crunchier cookies.

It seems that allergy-friendly goodies take longer to bake than your average baked goods. If you want to convert one of your own favorite recipes, make sure you watch the baking time. It usually takes 15 to 20 minutes longer for a cake and 5 to 10 minutes longer for cookies.

ORGANIZING TIPS

- Have all of your ingredients ready before you start baking. Line your baking sheets or grease them ahead of time.
- Sealed plastic containers help keep your goodies fresh and soft. Sometimes when cookies are exposed to air they lose their moisture and become too crunchy.
- If you have a child with severe food allergies, make a special spot in the kitchen, like a drawer or a cupboard, to store his ingredients and treats. Keep all of his items in large sealed plastic bags marked with stickers or writing. Teach your child that his safe goodies are in the special compartment. My daughter tapes up pictures of puppies and her drawings inside her special cupboard.

STORING YOUR GOODIES

Unless the directions indicate to store in the refrigerator, my suggestion is to keep cookies in an airtight resealable container like a cookie jar or tin. Most cookies and baked goods are at their peak of flavor within the first few days of baking. If you need to store cookies longer, I offer a few suggestions:

Biscotti and Scones: Store between layers of waxed paper in an airtight container. You may bake in the oven at 300°F (150°C, or gas mark 2) for 5 to 10 minutes or until warm. I do not recommend freezing.

Brownies: Wrap individually in plastic wrap or keep brownies in the baking pan and cover with plastic wrap. Freeze individually wrapped brownies for up to 3 months.

Candies: Store homemade candies like Chocolate-Covered Trail Mix Balls, Yum in a Haystack, 'Frigerator Fudge, and Flight-of-Fancy Florentines in a heavy-duty resealable plastic freezer bag. Try to remove as much air as possible and seal. Refrigerate for up to 10 days or freeze for up to 2 months.

Decorated or frosted cookies: Layer cookies between nonstick parchment paper and store in an airtight container. To freeze, wrap cookies individually in plastic wrap and gently place in a heavy-duty resealable plastic freezer bag, try to remove as much air as possible, and seal. Freeze up to 1 month. It is my suggestion to freeze cookies without decorations and frosting.

Drop cookies: Keep in an airtight container. To keep longer than 3 days, wrap in aluminum foil and keep in a cookie jar or tin. To freeze, wrap in aluminum foil, place in a heavy-duty resealable plastic freezer bag, try to remove as much air as possible, and seal. Freeze up to 3 months.

Fruit-filled bars: Wrap individually in plastic wrap or cover the baking pan with plastic wrap. Freeze for 1 month. Ludicrously Lemon Bars and Banana-danna Streusel Bars do not freeze well.

Other goodies: Store baked goods like fritters, pancakes, and muffins wrapped in aluminum foil or plastic wrap in an airtight container. Do not freeze.

Raw cookie dough: Place in a heavy-duty resealable plastic freezer bag, try to remove as much air as possible, and seal. Refrigerate for up to 3 days and freeze up to 2 months. Let defrost in the refrigerator.

Tarts: Place on a plate or container and wrap with aluminum foil or plastic wrap. Store in the refrigerator for a few days. To freeze, wrap tarts individually in plastic wrap and gently place in a heavy-duty resealable plastic freezer bag, try to remove as much air as possible, and seal. Freeze up to 1 month.

Chapter 5

Drop Cookies

Cookies, cookies! I have scanned the globe to
re-create cookies of all kinds   from healthy to sinful—and
make them allergy-friendly. Fruit-filled, fiber-packed,
flaky, "buttery," crunchy, chewy, gooey, hearty, or light,
you will find what you are looking for! These drop
cookies are really easy to make. Many of the following
cookies can be made with a small cookie scoop to make
the process a little faster.

Hearty Chocolate Chippers

1 cup (225 g) packed brown sugar

1/4 cup (60 ml) vegetable oil

1/4 cup (60 ml) water

1/2 cup (125 g) unsweetened
  applesauce

1/4 cup (28 g) flax meal

1 tablespoon (15 ml) vanilla extract

1 cup (125 g) Bob's Red Mill white or
  brown rice flour

1/2 cup (60 g) sorghum flour

1 teaspoon (4.6 g) baking soda

1/2 teaspoon (3 g) salt

2 cups (160 g) certified gluten-free
  rolled oats, quinoa, or rice flakes

1 cup (175 g) Enjoy Life semi-sweet
  chocolate chips or sulfite-free raisins

DIRECTIONS

- Preheat oven to 350°F (180°C, or gas mark 4).
- With a mixer or by hand, cream together the brown sugar, oil, water, applesauce, flax, and vanilla until smooth.
- Add the remaining ingredients except for the oats and chocolate chips, and mix until dough is well combined. Add the oats and mix again until all ingredients are combined. Stir in the chocolate chips.
- Use a small ice cream/cookie scoop or drop dough by rounded tablespoon onto a baking sheet. Flatten slightly.
- Bake for about 25 to 28 minutes, or until cookies are lightly browned and semi-soft to the touch in the middle. Let cookies sit for a few minutes before removing from baking sheet. Remove from baking sheet to a flat surface (like a large plate) or wire rack to cool completely before enjoying.

Yield: About 3 dozen

Oh-So-Delicious Sandwich Cookies

FOR COOKIES

¹⁄₂ cup (120 ml) vegetable oil

¹⁄₂ cup (120 ml) water

1 cup (200 g) superfine sugar

³⁄₄ cup (65 g) cocoa powder

¹⁄₂ teaspoon (3 g) salt

¹⁄₂ cup (60 g) Bob's Red Mill
   tapioca flour

2 cups (250 g) Bob's Red Mill white
   or brown rice flour or sorghum flour

¹⁄₄ teaspoon (1.2 g) baking powder

1 teaspoon (4.6 g) baking soda

¹⁄₃ cup (80 ml) water (optional)

FOR FILLING

¹⁄₂ cup (100 g) Spectrum
   Organic Shortening

2 cups (240 g) powdered sugar
   (contains cornstarch; can use
   corn-free recipe on page 43)

1 tablespoon (15 ml) vanilla extract

2 teaspoons (10 ml) rice milk, safe
   milk alternative, or water

DIRECTIONS

- Preheat oven to 350°F (180°C, or gas mark 4).
- To make the cookies: In a food processor, pulse together the oil, ¹⁄₂ cup (120 ml) water, sugar, cocoa, and salt. Add the flours, baking powder, and baking soda. Blend until dough forms a ball. If dough is too dry and is not forming into a ball, add the remaining ¹⁄₃ cup (80 ml) water a little at a time until a ball forms.
- Scoop out a 1-inch (2.5-cm) piece of dough and roll into a ball. Place 6 dough balls on a baking sheet lined with aluminum foil. Flatten evenly.
- Bake for 9 to 10 minutes, or until the tops appear crackled. Let cool on the baking sheet for 2 minutes. They should be firm like crackers, not super-soft. If they are too soft, bake for 5 more minutes. Once the cookies are the desired hardness, take a fork and make crisscrossing indentations on each cookie. Carefully lift each cookie off of the aluminum foil and cool on a flat surface or refrigerate.
- To make the filling: Place all filling ingredients in a food processor. Blend until smooth. The consistency should be thick like butter. If runny, add more powdered sugar. Frost the flat side of one cookie and top with another cookie.

Yield: About 2 dozen

Basically Yummy Cookie Dough

This super-easy dough is called for to make a variety of cookies.
Use it plain for a basic sugar cookie.

²/₃ cup (135 g) superfine sugar

¹/₂ cup (100 g) Spectrum
   Organic Shortening

2 teaspoons (10 ml) vanilla extract

¹/₂ cup (60 g) Bob's Red Mill
   tapioca flour

1 cup (125 g) Bob's Red Mill white
   rice flour

¹/₂ teaspoon (2.3 g) baking soda

¹/₄ (1.5 g) teaspoon salt

3 tablespoons (45 ml) rice milk,
   safe milk alternative, or water

DIRECTIONS

- Preheat oven to 350°F (180°C, or gas mark 4).
- In a food processor combine the sugar, shortening, and vanilla; pulse a few times to partially combine the ingredients. Add in the flours, baking soda, and salt. Pulse dough while slowly adding in the rice milk.
- Process until smooth (about 40 seconds). If necessary, add 1 teaspoon (5 ml) rice milk. Dough should look smooth but not firm. You should be able to pinch off a piece of dough and roll it into a soft ball without it sticking too much to your hands. If the dough appears watery, add in 1 tablespoon (8 g) powdered sugar or (7.8 g) rice flour at a time until the dough reaches the correct consistency.
- For sugar cookies, you can scoop with a small ice cream/cookie scoop or pinch off equal amounts of dough and roll into balls. Place on baking sheet 5 inches (13 cm) apart (about 6 cookies on an average-size baking sheet).
- Bake for about 15 minutes, or until cookies are slightly golden around the edges and have cracks on the tops. Even if they are not golden, when you see the cracks forming, remove from the oven. Let cool for one minute, then remove from baking sheet with a spatula and let cool completely on a flat surface.

Yield: About 3 dozen

Caramel-icious Apple Cookies

FOR COOKIES

½ cup (100 g) Spectrum
  Organic Shortening

1 ⅓ cups (300 g) packed brown sugar

2 cups (250 g) Bob's Red Mill white
  rice flour

½ cup (60 g) Bob's Red Mill
  tapioca flour

2 teaspoons (4.6 g) ground cinnamon

1 teaspoon (4.6 g) baking soda

½ teaspoon (3 g) salt

½ cup (120 ml) apple juice

½ cup (75 g) grated apple
  (1 small apple)

FOR CARAMEL ICING

1 ½ cups (180 g) powdered sugar
  (contains cornstarch; can use corn-
  free recipe on page 43)

½ cup (115 g) packed brown sugar

3 tablespoons (45 ml) rice milk, safe
  milk alternative, or water

DIRECTIONS

- Preheat oven to 350°F (180°C, or gas mark 4).
- To make the cookies: Cream together shortening and brown sugar. Add rice flour and next 5 ingredients (through apple juice) and mix until smooth. Stir in the grated apple.
- With a small ice cream/cookie scoop, drop dough onto a greased baking sheet (about 6 cookies per sheet).
- Bake for about 15 minutes, or until lightly golden. Let sit for 2 minutes before removing with a spatula to a flat surface. Let cool completely.
- To make the icing: Blend together all icing ingredients. Frost cooled cookies.

Yield: About 2 dozen

Crunch-tastic Molasses Cookies

3/4 cup (150 g) Spectrum
   Organic Shortening

1 cup (200 g) granulated sugar

1/4 cup (60 ml) water

1/4 cup (60 ml) unsulfured molasses

2 cups (250 g) Bob's Red Mill white
   rice flour

1/2 cup (60 g) Bob's Red Mill
   tapioca flour

2 teaspoons (9.2 g) baking soda

1 teaspoon (2.3 g) ground cinnamon

1/2 teaspoon (1 g) ground cloves

1 teaspoon (1.8 g) ground ginger

1/2 teaspoon (3 g) salt

1 cup (200 g) raw sugar or
   colored sugar

DIRECTIONS

- Preheat oven to 375°F (190°C, or gas mark 5).
- Melt the shortening in a saucepan on the stove, then remove from heat and set aside.
- With a mixer, combine the sugar, water, and molasses. Add the rice flour and the next 6 ingredients (through salt). Pour the melted shortening over the dry ingredients and start mixer on low. Scrape down the sides of the bowl, then turn mixer to medium speed and mix for 1 minute.
- Pinch off 1- to 2-inch (2.5- to 5-cm) pieces of dough and roll into balls. Place raw or colored sugar in a shallow bowl and roll each dough ball in sugar to coat. Place about 12 balls, evenly spaced, on a baking sheet.
- Bake for about 8 to 10 minutes. Let sit on the baking sheet for about 2 minutes before removing. Sprinkle with raw sugar if desired. With a flat spatula remove from the sheet to cool completely on a flat surface.

Yield: About 3 dozen

Chocolate Chip Harvest Cookies

This is a great treat all year long.

FOR COOKIES

2 cups (400 g) superfine sugar

1 cup (200 g) Spectrum
   Organic Shortening

1 can (15 ounce, or 427g) pumpkin

2 teaspoons (10 ml) vanilla extract

3 cups (375 g) Bob's Red Mill white or
   brown rice flour or sorghum flour

1 cup (125 g) Bob's Red Mill
   tapioca flour

2 teaspoons (9.2 g) baking soda

2 teaspoons (4.6 g) ground cinnamon

1 cup (175 g) Enjoy Life semi-sweet
   chocolate chips

FOR TOPPING

½ cup (85 g) Enjoy Life semi-sweet
   chocolate chips

DIRECTIONS

- Preheat oven to 375°F (190°C, or gas mark 5).
- To make the cookies: With a mixer, cream together the sugar, shortening, pumpkin, and vanilla. Add rice flour and next 3 ingredients (through cinnamon) and mix until smooth. Stir in chocolate chips.
- Drop by rounded tablespoon on a greased baking sheet. Bake for 12 to 15 minutes or until firm. With a spatula, remove cookies to a flat surface to cool completely.
- To make the topping: In a microwave-safe bowl, heat the chocolate chips at 30-second intervals until melted. Stir until completely smooth. Use a small spoon to drizzle melted chocolate in a crisscross pattern over each cookie. Let cool until chocolate drizzles have hardened.

Yield: About 4 dozen

Choco-Crazy Crinkle Cookies

A not-too-sweet-tasting and fun cookie for a special treat.

1 cup (200 g) granulated sugar

¼ cup (50 g) Spectrum
   Organic Shortening

2 teaspoons (10 ml) vanilla extract

½ cup (125 g) unsweetened
   applesauce

¾ cup (65 g) unsweetened
   cocoa powder

¼ cup (60 ml) water

⅓ cup (42 g) Bob's Red Mill
   tapioca flour

1 cup (125 g) Bob's Red Mill white
   or brown rice flour

½ teaspoon (2.3 g) baking soda

¼ teaspoon (1.5 g) salt

1 cup (120 g) powdered sugar
   (contains cornstarch; can use
   corn-free recipe on page 43)

DIRECTIONS

- Preheat oven to 350°F (180°C, or gas mark 4).
- With a mixer, add sugar, shortening, vanilla, applesauce, cocoa, and water. Mix until combined. Add in the tapioca flour and the next 3 ingredients (through salt) and mix until dough looks smooth but not firm, like cake batter.
- With an ice cream/cookie scoop, drop rounded balls of dough onto a greased cookie sheet. Use a spoon and sprinkle powdered sugar over cookie, coating heavily. Repeat with remaining cookies. You can put about 12 cookies on the baking sheet.
- Bake for about 15 minutes, or until cookies look slightly cracked. Let cool on the baking sheet for about 2 minutes before removing cookies to a cooling rack or flat surface to cool completely.

Yield: About 3 dozen

Snap 'em Up Ginger Snaps

Ginger snaps keep really well. Store some in a plastic bag in your car for a quick, crunchy treat on the go. Frost with the lemon icing, if desired.

FOR COOKIES

¾ cup (150 g) Spectrum
   Organic Shortening

¼ cup (60 ml) unsulfured molasses

1 cup (225 g) packed brown sugar

¼ cup (28 g) flax meal

Dash of salt

1 teaspoon (4.6 g) baking soda

1 teaspoon (1.8 g) ground ginger

1 teaspoon (2.3 g) ground cinnamon

1½ cups (185 g) Bob's Red Mill
   white rice flour

½ cup (50 g) rice bran

⅓ cup (42 g) Bob's Red Mill
   tapioca flour

5 teaspoons (25 ml) water

FOR ICING

1 cup (120 g) powdered sugar
   (contains cornstarch; can use corn-
   free recipe on page 43)

1 tablespoon (15 ml) lemon juice

DIRECTIONS

- Preheat oven to 350°F (180°C, or gas mark 4).
- To make the cookies: Cream together shortening, molasses, brown sugar, flax meal, and salt. Add in remaining cookie ingredients and blend until the dough forms into a ball. The dough will be dense.
- Pinch off dough and roll into 1-inch (2.5-cm) balls. Place about 12 cookies on a greased baking sheet. Flatten the cookies with a spatula.
- Bake for about 12 minutes, until middles are firm. Let cookies cool for 1 minute on baking sheet before removing with a spatula to a flat surface to cool completely.
- To make the icing: Mix powdered sugar and lemon juice until you reach a spreadable consistency. Drizzle over or frost cooled cookies.

Yield: About 4 dozen

Ginger-cake Cookies

Use this dough to make your Gingerbread men for the holidays.

FOR COOKIES

³/₄ cup (175 ml) unsulfured molasses

¹/₃ cup (75 g) packed brown sugar

¹/₃ cup (80 ml) water

2 tablespoons (30 ml) vegetable oil

Dash of salt

2 ¹/₄ cups (280 g) Bob's Red Mill
   white or brown rice flour

1 cup (125 g) Bob's Red Mill
   tapioca flour

1 teaspoon (4.6 g) baking soda

¹/₂ teaspoon (1 g) ground allspice

1 teaspoon (1.8 g) ground ginger

¹/₂ teaspoon (1 g) ground cloves

¹/₂ teaspoon (1.2 g) ground cinnamon

FOR FROSTING

1 cup (120 g) powdered sugar
   (contains cornstarch; can use corn-
   free recipe on page 43)

2 teaspoons (10 ml) rice milk, safe
   milk alternative, or water

1 teaspoon (5 ml) vanilla extract

DIRECTIONS

- Preheat oven to 350°F (180°C, or gas mark 4).
- To make the cookies: With a mixer, cream together molasses, brown sugar, water, oil, and salt. Add remaining cookie ingredients and mix well.
- Use a large ice cream/cookie scoop or drop dough by rounded tablespoon onto a greased baking sheet and flatten slightly. Or, to make cut-out cookies, divide dough in half and pat each half into a disk. Roll each disk into an even ½-inch (1.2-cm) thick circle. Use your favorite cookie cutters to cut out shapes from the dough. Place each cookie shape onto a greased baking sheet.
- Bake for about 12 to 15 minutes, or until golden around the edges and puffy in the middle. Let cool for 2 minutes on the baking sheet before removing to cool completely on a flat surface.
- To make the frosting: Mix together the powdered sugar, vanilla, and "milk" and frost the cooled cookies.

Yield: About 2 dozen

AN OPPORTUNITY TO DISCOVER A NEW TALENT

Mary Esselman Roberts

When you first get the food allergy diagnosis, you don't quite get how it's going to change your life. We understood that we needed to get rid of the peanut butter, the walnuts, and the almonds. It took us a while to figure out that the old jellies and jams in our fridge needed to go (cross-contaminated), and that the old oil-seasoned cookie sheets and skillets were no longer safe. Then we started to "get" that we needed to call manufacturers to be sure certain basic ingredients weren't processed on lines with nuts or seeds. And finally, I realized that life would change beyond our kitchen, outside of the home.

Food would become a source of tension, a constant burden, an enemy to be defeated. Family gatherings went from fun to stressful ("No, we can't eat that lovingly made casserole . . . I'm sure you were careful, sorry to hurt your feelings, but no we won't try those cookies."). Potlucks with friends became as relaxing as a stroll through a minefield. Play dates and parties, travel and celebrations—I wanted my son to enjoy all of these things, to be normal. But each invitation, each plan to go somewhere left me exhausted and sad before I even started. What to make; how to pack it; what to say to people; how to stay vigilant but calm, careful but pleasant; how to not let my heart break a little when my son had to settle for his cupcake while the other kids were tearing into the really cool spaceship/race car/whatever cake.

I still find it tiring and stressful to manage our multiple food allergies. However, I think I'm slowly starting to rise to this challenge. I was a terrible cook/baker before my son was born (I ate out just about every meal), and now, I can pull off a decent meal here and there. As for baking, I have to say I'm proud of myself. I bake! My husband and son rave! Breads, brownies, cupcakes, and cookies! They may not be fancy, but they're tasty and healthy—and healthy is a big deal to me now. I use very few processed ingredients, and no preservatives, additives, or artificial colors. It took time, but I've learned how to make delicious food that we all enjoy, that I can freeze and pack, and that I can cart to our social gatherings with a minimum of hassle. The best part? Knowing we have food good enough to share with others. I am thrilled when my son can proudly offer gooey brownies or crispy cookies to his friends. The kids don't know that the goodies are allergen-free, and my son gets to share something he enjoys with others. Here's a cookie recipe we love: **3 ripe bananas; 2 cups (160 g) certified gluten-free oats; 1 ½ cups (210 g) mixed dried fruit; 1 teaspoon (5 ml) vanilla**

DIRECTIONS Preheat oven to 350°F (180°C, or gas mark 4). Mash bananas in large bowl. Add other ingredients; mix. Drop by spoonfuls on an ungreased cookie sheet. Bake for approximately 20 minutes.

Hardly Crabby Hermit Cookies

This has become my favorite cookie.

½ cup (100 g) Spectrum Organic Shortening

½ cup (125 g) unsweetened applesauce

1 ½ cups (345 g) packed brown sugar

2 ½ cups (310 g) Bob's Red Mill white or brown rice flour

1 cup (125 g) Bob's Red Mill tapioca flour

1 teaspoon (4.6 g) baking soda

1 teaspoon (6 g) salt

1 teaspoon (2.2 g) ground nutmeg

1 teaspoon (2.3 g) ground cinnamon

½ cup (120 ml) unsweetened apple juice

2 cups (330 g) packed sulfite-free raisins

½ cup (114 g) pumpkin seed kernels

DIRECTIONS

- Preheat oven to 375°F (190°C, or gas mark 5).
- Cream together shortening, applesauce, and brown sugar. Add the rice flour and the next 6 ingredients (through the apple juice). Mix together until you have a smooth batter. Stir in the raisins and pumpkin seeds.
- Drop dough by rounded teaspoonful onto a greased baking sheet. Bake for about 12 minutes, or until cookies are semi-firm in the centers. Remove to a flat surface to cool.

Yield: About 3 dozen

Island Sunshine Cookies

1 cup (200 g) Spectrum
  Organic Shortening
1 cup (200 g) superfine sugar
3 ½ cups (435 g) Bob's Red Mill white
  or brown rice flour
1 cup (125 g) Bob's Red Mill
  tapioca flour

1 teaspoon (4.6 g) baking soda
½ teaspoon (3 g) salt
¼ teaspoon (0.6 g) ground
  nutmeg (optional)
1 cup (250 g) canned crushed
  pineapple with juice

DIRECTIONS

- Preheat oven to 375°F (190°C, or gas mark 5).
- With a mixer, cream together the shortening and the sugar. Add the remaining ingredients except the pineapple and mix briefly. Stir in the pineapple until combined.
- Drop dough by rounded teaspoonfuls onto a greased baking sheet. Bake for about 12 minutes, or until cookies are firm to the touch. Let cool on the baking sheet for 2 minutes before removing to a flat surface to cool completely. Dust with powdered sugar (or corn-free recipe on page 43), if desired.

Yield: About 3 dozen

Positively Pumpkin Cookies

*Not just for the fall season, these nutritious cookies let you enjoy the
flavors of autumn all year long.*

1 cup (225 g) packed brown sugar

1 teaspoon (5 ml) vanilla extract

$\frac{1}{2}$ cup (125 g) unsweetened
applesauce

$\frac{1}{4}$ cup (60 ml) vegetable oil

$\frac{1}{2}$ teaspoon (3 g) salt

1 cup (245 g) canned pumpkin

1 cup (125 g) Bob's Red Mill brown
rice flour or sorghum flour

$\frac{1}{2}$ cup (56 g) flax meal

$\frac{1}{2}$ cup (50 g) rice bran

1 teaspoon (2.3 g) ground cinnamon

1 teaspoon (4.6 g) baking soda

1 cup (165 g) packed sulfite-
free raisins

1 cup (150 g) chopped apple, very
small pieces (about 1 small apple)

DIRECTIONS

- Preheat oven to 350°F (180°C, or gas mark 4).
- With a mixer ,combine the brown sugar, vanilla, applesauce, oil, and salt. Add the pumpkin and the next 5 ingredients (through baking soda) and mix until you have a smooth, semi-firm dough. By hand, stir in the raisins and apple pieces.
- Drop dough by rounded tablespoon onto a baking sheet. Flatten slightly. Bake for about 20 to 25 minutes, or until cookies are firm and lightly browned. Let cool on the baking sheet for 2 minutes, then remove to a flat surface or wire rack to cool completely.

Yield: About 3 dozen

Thumbs Up Thumbprint Cookies

When I was a child my mom let me poke my thumb in the center and fill the cookies with my favorite jams. They are allergy-friendly for everyone's enjoyment!

FOR COOKIES

²/₃ cup (135 g) superfine sugar

½ cup (100 g) Spectrum Organic Shortening

2 teaspoons (10 ml) vanilla extract

½ cup (60 g) Bob's Red Mill tapioca flour

1 cup (125 g) Bob's Red Mill white rice flour

1 teaspoon (4.6 g) baking powder

¼ teaspoon (1.5 g) salt

3 tablespoons (45 ml) rice milk, safe milk alternative, or water

FOR TOPPING

1 cup (80 g) certified gluten-free rolled oats, or quinoa or rice flakes

1 cup (320 g) of your favorite safe jam

DIRECTIONS

- Preheat oven to 350°F (180°C, or gas mark 4).
- To make the cookies: With a mixer, partially combine the sugar, shortening, and vanilla. Add in the dry ingredients. Mix on low while slowly adding in the milk.
- The dough should look smooth but not firm. You should be able to pinch off a piece and roll it into a soft ball without it sticking too much to your hands. If the dough appears watery, add in 1 tablespoon (8 g) powdered sugar at a time until the dough reaches the correct consistency. If the dough is too dry, add 1 teaspoon (5 ml) of rice milk.
- Pinch off about 1 tablespoon (16 g) of dough and roll into balls. Set aside.
- To make the topping: In a food processor or coffee grinder, grind the oats into a coarse consistency like oat bran. Place in a shallow bowl.
- Roll dough balls in the oats and coat well. Place coated balls on a baking sheet. Using your thumb or two fingers, create a shallow, even indentation in each ball. Fill with about 1 teaspoon (7 g) of jam.
- Bake for about 15 minutes, or until edges are golden. Let cool for about 10 minutes on baking sheet before removing to a flat surface to cool completely.

Yield: About 3 dozen

Cinnabar Swirl Cookies

A swirl of ground cinnamon in a moist apple cookie brings delight to the senses.
The flavor reminds me of a not-too-sweet cinnamon roll.

1 cup (245 g) unsweetened
  applesauce
½ cup (120 ml) vegetable oil
2 teaspoons (10 ml) vanilla extract
1 ¼ cups (285 g) packed dark
  brown sugar
Dash of salt
2 cups (250 g) Bob's Red Mill white
  or brown rice flour
⅔ cup (80 g) Bob's Red Mill
  tapioca flour

1 tablespoon (7 g) plus 1 teaspoon
  (2.3 g) ground cinnamon, divided
1 teaspoon (1.8 g) ground ginger
1 tablespoon (14 g) baking powder
2 cups (250 g) coarsely grated apples
  (about 4 medium)
1 cup (165 g) packed golden or
  regular sulfite-free raisins
Ground cinnamon

DIRECTIONS

- Preheat oven to 350°F (180°C, or gas mark 4).
- With a mixer, cream together applesauce, oil, vanilla, brown sugar, and salt. Add in flours, 1 teaspoon (2.3 g) cinnamon, ginger, and baking powder and blend until smooth. Stir in the apples and raisins.
- Let dough sit for about 3 minutes. Spoon the remaining 1 tablespoon (7 g) cinnamon onto the center of the dough. Using the mixer, gently blend the cinnamon into the dough without overmixing (leave streaks of cinnamon throughout the mixture).
- Drop dough by heaping tablespoon onto a baking sheet, 6 per sheet. Bake for 15 to 20 minutes, or until golden around the bottoms. Let cool for 2 minutes on the baking sheet before removing to a flat surface to cool completely.

Yield: About 3 dozen

Two-Tone Temptations Cookies

$^2/_3$ cup (135 g) superfine sugar

$^1/_2$ cup (100 g) Spectrum
  Organic Shortening

2 teaspoons (10 ml) vanilla extract

$^1/_2$ cup (60 g) Bob's Red Mill
  tapioca flour

1 cup (125 g) Bob's Red Mill white
  rice flour

$^1/_2$ teaspoon (2.3 g) baking soda

$^1/_4$ teaspoon (1.5 g) salt

2 to 3 tablespoons (30 to 45 ml) rice
  milk, safe milk alternative, or water

1 cup (175 g) Enjoy Life semi-sweet
  chocolate chips

DIRECTIONS

- Preheat oven to 350°F (180°C, or gas mark 4).
- With a mixer, cream together the sugar, shortening, and vanilla to partially combine ingredients. Add in the tapioca flour and the next 3 ingredients (through salt). Mix on low while slowly adding in the rice milk.
- Dough should look smooth but not firm. If the dough appears watery, add in 1 tablespoon (8 g) powdered sugar at a time until the dough reaches the correct consistency. If dough is too dry, add 1 teaspoon (5 ml) of additional rice milk.
- Scoop dough with a small ice cream/cookie scoop or pinch off equal amounts of dough and roll into balls. Place on a baking sheet 5 inches (12.5 cm) apart (about 6 cookies on an average-size baking sheet). Flatten dough evenly.
- Bake for about 15 minutes, or until cookies are slightly golden around edges and have cracks on the tops. Even if they are not golden, when you see the cracks forming the cookies, remove them from the oven. Let cool for 1 minute, then remove from baking sheet with a spatula and cool completely on a flat surface.
- In a deep and narrow microwave-proof bowl, heat the chocolate chips at 30-second intervals, stirring at each interval, until melted. Stir until smooth. Dip half of each cooled cookie into the melted chocolate. Lay cookies on a baking sheet lined with nonstick parchment paper or aluminum foil. Let cool completely.

Yield: About 3 dozen

Persimmon Perfection Cookies

Where I live, during the fall persimmons are available on trees outside and in my local grocery store. If you live in an area where persimmons are not available, try searching for an online vendor or at an Asian grocery store. This fruit is a real treat and is worth searching for; I love persimmon cookies and breads on a chilly fall night! You may replace persimmon pulp with puréed peaches if you cannot find persimmons.

FOR COOKIES

½ cup (100 g) Spectrum
 Organic Shortening

1 cup (200 g) superfine sugar

¼ cup (28 g) flax meal

1 cup (245 g) persimmon pulp
 (or peach purée)

2 cups (250 g) Bob's Red Mill brown
 or white rice flour

½ cup (60 g) Bob's Red Mill
 tapioca flour

½ teaspoon (2.3 g) baking powder

½ teaspoon (2.3 g) baking soda

½ teaspoon (1.2 g) ground cinnamon

¼ teaspoon (0.5 g) ground cloves

½ teaspoon (3 g) salt

½ cup (80 g) sulfite-free raisins
 or cranberries

FOR ICING

½ cup (60 g) powdered sugar
 (contains cornstarch; can use corn-
 free recipe on page 43)

1 teaspoon (5 ml) water

DIRECTIONS

- Preheat oven to 350°F (180°C, or gas mark 4).
- To make the cookies: With a mixer, cream together the shortening, sugar, flax, and persimmon pulp. Mix in the rice flour and the next 6 ingredients (through salt). Stir in the raisins or cranberries.
- Use a small ice cream/cookie scoop or drop dough by rounded tablespoon onto a baking sheet, about 6 per average-sized baking sheet. Flatten slightly.
- Bake for about 20 minutes, or until edges are firm. Let cool on baking sheet for 1 minute before removing to a flat surface with a spatula to cool completely.
- To make the icing: In a bowl, mix together the powdered sugar and water. Add more water as needed to reach desired consistency. Drizzle icing over cookies in a zigzag pattern.

Yield: About 3 dozen

RECIPE NOTE

How to make persimmon pulp: Store ripe persimmons in the refrigerator. Remove and let stand at room temperature for about 1 hour. Peel persimmons or scrape pulp from peel with a spoon. Press persimmons through a fine mesh strainer, or mash with a fork.

Light 'n Lacy Oatmeal Crisps

These cookies are very delicate, and the flavor is reminiscent of butterscotch. They remind me of a caramel candy treat.

³/₄ cup (170 g) firmly packed
   brown sugar
½ cup (100 g) Spectrum
   Organic Shortening
2 tablespoons (90 ml) vanilla extract

¼ teaspoon (1.5 g) salt
1 ¼ cups (100 g) certified gluten-free
   rolled oat or rice flakes
2 tablespoons (15 g) oat flour or
   Bob's Red Mill tapioca flour

DIRECTIONS

- Preheat oven to 350°F (180°C, or gas mark 4).
- With a mixer, cream together the brown sugar, shortening, vanilla, and salt for about 1 minute. Add the oats and flour and mix until well combined.
- Line a baking sheet with aluminum foil or nonstick parchment paper. Drop the dough by level teaspoonful onto baking sheet. Space them out well because they will spread (about 6 per baking sheet).
- Bake for 8 to 12 minutes or until cookies are golden brown around the edges. Using a hot pad, gently slide the foil or parchment paper off the baking sheet and onto a flat surface. Let cookies cool completely before carefully removing (the cookies are easily breakable). Freeze on a flat surface before eating, if desired.

Yield: About 2 dozen

Sensational Snickerdoodle Cookies

These cookies are a simple treat for anyone who loves ground cinnamon.
My youngest prefers these cookies to anything chocolate.

²/₃ cup (135 g) superfine sugar

¹/₃ cup (80 ml) vegetable oil

2 teaspoons (10 ml) vanilla extract

¹/₂ cup (60 g) Bob's Red Mill
  tapioca flour

1 cup (125 g) Bob's Red Mill white
  rice flour

¹/₂ teaspoon (2.3 g) cream of tartar

¹/₂ teaspoon (2.3 g) baking powder

¹/₄ teaspoon (1.5 g) salt

1 tablespoon (15 ml) rice milk, safe
  milk alternative, or water

¹/₂ cup (100 g) raw sugar

1 tablespoon (7 g) ground cinnamon

DIRECTIONS

- Preheat oven to 350°F (180°C, or gas mark 4).
- In a food processor, add the sugar, oil, and vanilla and pulse a few times to partially combine ingredients. Add in the tapioca flour and the next 4 ingredients (through salt). Pulse dough while slowly adding in the rice milk.
- Process until smooth (about 40 seconds). Dough should look smooth but not firm. You should be able to pinch off a piece of dough and roll it into a soft ball without the dough sticking to your hands. If the dough appears watery, add in 1 tablespoon (8 g) powdered sugar at a time until dough reaches correct consistency. If dough is too dry, add 1 teaspoon (5 ml) of additional rice milk.
- Pinch off about 1 to 2 teaspoons (5 to 10 g) of dough at a time and roll into balls.
- Combine the sugar and cinnamon in a shallow bowl. Place a dough ball in the sugar mixture. With a spoon, sprinkle sugar mixture over the surface of the cookie.
- Place dough balls onto a baking sheet (about 10 per baking sheet). Flatten slightly. If desired, sprinkle more sugar mixture on top of each flattened cookie.
- Bake for 8 to 12 minutes or until cookies are golden brown around the edges. Remove with a spatula to a flat surface or wire rack to cool completely.

Yield: About 2 dozen

Glorious Glazed Citrus Cookies

These cookies are very delicate, and the flavor is awesome!

FOR COOKIES

½ cup (100 g) Spectrum
   Organic Shortening

½ cup (100 g) superfine sugar

¼ cup (60 ml) lemon or lime juice

1 teaspoon (1.7 g) grated lemon
   or lime zest

1 ½ cups (185 g) Bob's Red Mill white
   rice flour

½ teaspoon (2.3 g) baking powder

½ cup (65 g) cornstarch (contains
   corn; can use tapioca or arrowroot
   starch instead)

FOR GLAZE

1 cup (120 g) powdered sugar
   (contains cornstarch; can use corn-
   free recipe on page 43)

3 tablespoons (45 ml) lemon
   or lime juice

DIRECTIONS

- Preheat oven to 350°F (180°C, or gas mark 4).
- To make the cookies: Mix the shortening, sugar, juice, and zest. Mixture will look coagulated. Add the remaining cookie ingredients, blend until the dough is smooth.
- Form dough into a ball, cover in plastic wrap, and refrigerate for 30 minutes. If dough becomes too firm from being too chilled, leave out at room temperature for a few minutes until dough is easier to work with.
- Pinch off 1 to 2 teaspoons (5 to 10 g) of dough and roll into a ball. Place on a baking sheet about 2 inches apart (5 cm). Do not flatten.
- Bake for about 15 minutes, or until cookies are golden around the bottom edges. Remove with a spatula and place on a flat surface to cool.
- To make the glaze: Mix powdered sugar and juice until smooth.
- While the cookies are warm, spoon glaze over each cookie. After the cookies are cooled completely, spread an additional thin layer of glaze on each cookie, if you desire. Put on a flat surface and place in the refrigerator to harden the glaze.
- If you do not want to use the glaze, roll the cooled cookies in powdered sugar.

Yield: About 3 dozen

Munchy Crunch Cookies

1 cup (200 g) superfine sugar

1 cup (225 g) packed brown sugar

1 cup (245 g) unsweetened
applesauce

1 cup (235 ml) vegetable oil

1 tablespoon (15 ml) vanilla extract

1/4 cup (28 g) flax meal

1 teaspoon (4.6 g) cream of tartar

1 cup (125 g) Bob's Red Mill
tapioca flour

2 cups (250 g) Bob's Red Mill brown
or white rice flour

1/2 cup (50 g) rice bran or
sorghum flour

1 teaspoon (6 g) salt

1 teaspoon (4.6 g) baking soda

1/4 cup (34 g) sunflower seed kernels

1 1/2 cups (110 g) Enjoy Life Perky's
"Nutty" Rice or "Nutty" Flax cereal

1 cup (80 g) certified gluten-free
rolled oats or rice flakes

2/3 cup (117 g) Enjoy Life semi-sweet
chocolate chips (optional)

DIRECTIONS

- Preheat oven to 350°F (180°C, or gas mark 4).
- With a mixer, combine the sugars, applesauce, oil, vanilla, and flax meal. Add the cream of tartar and the next 5 ingredients (through baking soda) and mix well. Stir in the sunflower seeds, cereal, and oats. Stir in the chocolate chips, if desired.
- Drop dough by rounded tablespoon on a baking sheet, about 6 cookies per baking sheet. Bake for about 20 minutes, or until golden around the edges. Let cool 1 minute on baking sheet before removing with a spatula to a flat surface to cool completely.

Yield: About 3 dozen

People's Choice Chocolate Chip Cookies

These are good warm out of the oven and great the next day.

1/3 cup (80 ml) vegetable oil

1 cup (225 g) packed brown sugar

2 teaspoons (10 ml) vanilla extract

1/4 teaspoon (1.5 g) salt

1 cup (125 g) Bob's Red Mill white
   rice flour

1/2 cup (60 g) Bob's Red Mill
   tapioca flour

1 teaspoon (4.6 g) baking powder

1/4 cup plus 2 tablespoons
   (90 ml) water

1 cup (175 g) Enjoy Life semi-sweet
   chocolate chips

DIRECTIONS

- Preheat oven to 350°F (180°C, or gas mark 4).
- With a mixer, or by hand, stir together oil, brown sugar, vanilla, and salt. Add the flours and baking powder and mix on low speed. While mixing, slowly pour in the water until the dough is smooth. Stir in the chocolate chips.
- Use a small ice cream/cookie scoop or drop dough by tablespoon onto a baking sheet, spacing the cookies about 2 inches (5 cm) apart (about 6 cookies per baking sheet).
- Bake for 12 to 15 minutes. Cookies will be golden around the edges and soft in the center. For softer cookies, remove from oven before they get too golden—around 12 minutes. Let cool on baking sheet for less than 1 minute. Remove with a flat spatula and place on a flat surface to cool completely.

Yield: About 2 dozen

Chock-o Chocolate Chunks Cookies

⅓ cup (80 ml) vegetable oil

1 cup (225 g) packed brown sugar

1 tablespoon (15 ml) vanilla extract

¼ teaspoon (1.5 g) salt

1 cup (125 g) Bob's Red Mill white
rice flour

½ cup (65 g) cornstarch (contains
corn; can use tapioca or arrowroot
starch instead)

1 teaspoon (4.6 g) baking powder

¼ cup (60 ml) water

3 (1.4-ounce, or 40-g) Enjoy Life
boom CHOCO boom dark chocolate bars, chopped into 1-inch
(2.5-cm) chunks

DIRECTIONS

- Preheat oven to 350°F (180°C, or gas mark 4).
- With a mixer combine the oil, brown sugar, vanilla, and salt. Add the flour, starch, and baking powder and mix on low speed. While mixing, slowly pour in the water until the dough is smooth. Stir in the chocolate chunks.
- Use a small ice cream/cookie scoop or drop dough by tablespoon onto a baking sheet, spacing the cookies about 2 inches (5 cm) apart (about 6 cookies per baking sheet).
- Bake for about 12 to 15 minutes, or until cookies are golden around the edges and soft in the center. For softer cookies, remove from oven before they get too golden—around 12 minutes. Let cool on the baking sheet for less than 1 minute. Remove with a flat spatula and place on a flat surface to cool completely.

Yield: About 2 dozen

Banana Choco-Chunk Drops

3 ripe bananas

½ cup (100 g) Spectrum Organic Shortening

1 cup (225 g) packed brown sugar

¼ cup (60 ml) rice milk

3 cups (240 g) certified gluten-free oats or rice flakes

3 tablespoons (24 g) Bob's Red Mill tapioca flour

½ cup (60 g) Bob's Red Mill white rice flour

1 ½ teaspoons (7 g) baking soda

½ teaspoon (3 g) salt

1 teaspoon (5 ml) vanilla extract

3 (1.4-ounce, or 40-g) Enjoy Life boom CHOCO boom dark chocolate bars, chopped into 1-inch (2.5-cm) chunks

¼ cup (34 g) salted sunflower seed kernels or 1 cup (140 g) Enjoy Life Not Nuts! Beach Bash or Mountain Mambo trail mix

DIRECTIONS

- Preheat oven to 350°F (180°C, or gas mark 4).
- With a mixer, cream together bananas, shortening, and brown sugar. Add in rice milk and next 6 ingredients (through vanilla) and blend until smooth. Stir in the chocolate chunks and seeds.
- Drop batter by tablespoon onto a baking sheet. Batter will look very wet.
- Bake for 15 minutes. Let cool on the baking sheet for 2 minutes, then remove with a spatula to a flat surface to cool completely.

Yield: About 4 dozen

A FAMILY'S NEW DIET BRINGS NEW HOPES

Jane M. Roberts

Six years ago, I delivered my third child. No one (especially me!) could have imagined what lay ahead. After Andrew was born, I had some health complications that meant an early introduction to formula. During Andrew's first months, he had rashes and blood in his stool and was constantly vomiting. Finally, my pediatrician suggested a prescription formula based on a suspicion of a dairy allergy. During this time, my daughter Emily, age four, had developed very serious rashes and concerning behaviors. Then Emily stopped speaking—a skill she had mastered at the early age of one! She was diagnosed with PDD/NOS (Pervasive Developmental Delay/Not Otherwise Specified), which was later diagnosed as high-functioning autism.

My middle child, Claire, age two, was classified as failure to thrive (she was significantly underweight) and had chronic diarrhea. After frantically trying to help my children get healthy and reading anything I could about food allergies and autism, I heard about the gluten-free/casein-free (GFCF) diet. My children's pediatrician pooh-poohed it, but I tried it anyway and found a new doctor for them.

When we relocated to North Carolina, we found a wonderful pediatrician who tested the whole family for Celiac Disease. Lo and behold, all five of us (my husband included) have it! I had the children tested, and it turned out they were allergic to everything under the sun! Peanuts, tree nuts, eggs, dairy, and soy, just to name a few. The kids did endoscopies and other tests. Claire had to have surgery for the valves to her kidneys to work better. It was a scary and trying time.

The whole family adopted the GFCF diet, and we saw dramatic changes. Emily's speech came back, Claire started to grow, and Andrew's rashes went away. My joint pain disappeared. Back then, I was boiling bagels, rolling my own pizzas, and dreaming of a day that my kids could have a cereal that even looked liked Cheerios. I was running from occupational therapist to child psychologist and hoping for a break.

One day, when Emily was five, her kindergarten teacher called and asked if I had anything like gluten-free fortune cookies for her. I rolled that dough and brought in the funniest looking fortune cookie ever! Now, that has all changed. We can go to the local grocery store and buy the kids safe cookies that taste delicious, and I don't have to boil my own bagels anymore either because of the allergy-friendly products that are available now! We stuck with our celiac and allergen-free diet. Over the years, the kids have grown out of many of their allergies. We have a lingering nut allergy, but after six years of mixing baking soda and water to try to make imitation egg, we'll take it.

Mighty Mini-Chip Snowballs

A melt-in-your-mouth treat with a chocolate chip twist.

½ cup (100 g) Spectrum Organic Shortening

½ cup (60 g) Bob's Red Mill white rice flour

½ cup (65 g) cornstarch (contains corn; can use arrowroot starch instead)

½ cup (60 g) powdered sugar (contains cornstarch; can use corn-free recipe on page 43)

⅛ teaspoon (0.6 g) baking powder

⅛ teaspoon (0.8 g) salt

1 teaspoon (5 ml) vanilla

1 cup (175 g) Enjoy Life semi-sweet chocolate chips

1 cup (120 g) powdered sugar (contains cornstarch; can use corn-free recipe on page 43)

DIRECTIONS

- Preheat oven to 350°F (180°C, or gas mark 4).
- In a food processor, combine shortening and next 6 ingredients (through vanilla) and process for 1 minute. Add chocolate chips and pulse a few times.
- Roll dough into 1-inch (2.5-cm) balls. Place on a greased baking sheet.
- Bake for about 10 minutes, or until edges are golden. Sift powdered sugar over warm cookies. Remove to a flat surface to let cool completely. If desired, sprinkle cooled cookies with additional powdered sugar.

Yield: About 5 dozen

Super Sunflower Crunch Cookies

These crunchy cookies are popular with children of all ages.

1 cup (260 g) sunflower butter

1 cup (200 g) sugar

1 teaspoon (5 ml) vanilla extract

3 tablespoons (45 ml) vegetable oil

1 cup (125 g) Bob's Red Mill white or
brown rice flour

¼ cup (30 g) Bob's Red Mill
tapioca flour

Dash of salt

½ teaspoon (2.3 g) baking powder

⅓ cup (45 g) sunflower seed kernels

2 tablespoons (26 g) raw sugar
(optional)

DIRECTIONS

- Preheat oven to 350°F (180°C, or gas mark 4).
- Cream together sunflower butter, sugar, and vanilla. Mix in oil and next 4 ingredients (through baking powder). Stir in sunflower seeds.
- Use a small scoop to drop dough onto a greased baking sheet (about 6 cookies per baking sheet). Flatten slightly. Sprinkle each cookie with raw sugar, if desired.
- Bake for about 20 minutes. Remove to a flat surface to cool completely.

Yield: About 3 dozen

RECIPE NOTE

Have you ever noticed a green discoloration in your baked goods made with sunflower butter? No alarm! This discoloration occurs when sunflower butter is used in combination with baking soda or baking powder. Sunflower seeds are rich in chlorogenic acid, which is found naturally in all plants. Most plants only have chlorogenic acid in their stems and leaves, but sunflowers also contain it in their seeds. This is one of the reasons sunflower is so good for you!

Go to www.sunbutter.com/cookingtips.asp for more info!

Jammin' Jive Cookies

½ cup (100 g) Spectrum Organic Shortening

½ cup (60 g) Bob's Red Mill white rice flour

½ cup (65 g) cornstarch (contains corn; can use arrowroot starch instead)

½ cup (60 g) powdered sugar (contains cornstarch; can use corn-free recipe on page 43)

⅛ teaspoon (0.6 g) baking powder

⅛ teaspoon (0.8 g) salt

1 teaspoon (5 ml) vanilla

1 cup (320 g) "safe" jam, such as apricot, strawberry, raspberry, blueberry, blackberry, or currant

DIRECTIONS

- Preheat oven to 350°F (180°C, or gas mark 4).
- In a food processor, combine shortening and next 6 ingredients (through vanilla) and process for 1 minute.
- Using your hands, roll dough into 2-inch (5-cm) balls and place on a greased baking sheet (about 10 cookies per baking sheet). With your thumb or two fingers, make an indentation in the top of each dough ball. Fill with 1 teaspoon (7 g) of jam.
- Bake for about 15 minutes, or until edges are golden. Let cookies sit for 2 minutes on baking sheet, then remove to a flat surface and let cool completely.

Yield: About 3 dozen

RECIPE NOTE

Recipe does not work well with blended flour mix.

Hearty Choco Choco Chippers

A melt-in-your-mouth treat with a chocolate chip twist.

1/2 cup (125 g) unsweetened
   applesauce

1/2 cup (120 ml) vegetable oil

1 teaspoon (6 g) salt

2 teaspoons (10 ml) vanilla extract

2/3 cup (135 g) granulated sugar

2/3 cup (150 g) firmly packed
   brown sugar

1/4 cup (22 g) unsweetened
   cocoa powder

1 1/4 cups (156 g) sorghum flour

1/2 cup (60 g) Bob's Red Mill white
   or brown rice flour

1/2 cup (60 g) Bob's Red Mill
   tapioca flour

1 teaspoon (4.6 g) baking soda

1 1/2 cups (265 g) Enjoy Life
   semi-sweet chocolate chips

DIRECTIONS

- Preheat oven to 350°F (180°C, or gas mark 4).
- Cream together applesauce, oil, salt, vanilla, sugars, and cocoa. Add in flours and baking soda. Stir in chocolate chips.
- Use a small ice cream/cookie scoop to drop dough onto a baking sheet.
- Bake for about 15 minutes. Remove cookies from baking sheet and let cool on a flat surface.

Yield: About 3 dozen

Sun and Moon Cookies

A "nutty"-flavored cookie dipped in chocolate.

⅓ cup (80 ml) vegetable oil

½ cup (130 g) sunflower butter

½ cup (115 g) packed brown sugar

1 teaspoon (5 ml) vanilla extract

½ teaspoon (2.3 g) baking soda

½ teaspoon (2.3 g) baking powder

¼ cup (30 g) Bob's Red Mill tapioca flour

1 cup (125 g) Bob's Red Mill white or brown rice flour

1 cup (175 g) Enjoy Life semi-sweet chocolate chips

DIRECTIONS

- Preheat oven to 375°F (190°C, or gas mark 5).
- With a mixer, cream together oil, sunflower butter, brown sugar, and vanilla. Add baking soda, baking powder, and flours and mix well.
- Use a small ice cream/cookie scoop or drop dough by rounded tablespoon onto a baking sheet.
- Bake for about 15 minutes, or until edges are golden and the centers are soft and puffy. Let sit on baking sheet for 2 minutes before removing with a spatula to a flat surface to cool completely.
- In a deep and narrow microwave-proof bowl, heat chocolate chips at 30-second intervals, stirring at each interval, until melted. Stir until smooth. Dip half of each cooled cookie into the melted chocolate. Lay cookie on a baking sheet lined with nonstick parchment paper or aluminum foil. Let cool completely (you may place in the refrigerator to speed up the hardening of the chocolate).

Yield: About 2 dozen

Cookies on a Stick

FOR COOKIES

1 recipe Fantastic Fairy Cookie
 dough (page 90)

18 wooden cookie sticks

FOR DECORATIONS

1 cup (170 g) "safe" candy, Enjoy Life
 boom CHOCO boom chocolate bar
 (melted, chopped or both) or semi-
 sweet chocolate chips, or colored
 sugar

FOR FROSTING

¼ cup (50 g) Spectrum
 Organic Shortening

1 teaspoon (5 ml) vanilla extract

2 cups (240 g) powdered sugar
 (contains cornstarch, can use corn-
 free recipe on page #)

1 tablespoon (15 ml) water

Dash of salt

DIRECTIONS

- Preheat oven to 350°F (180°C, or gas mark 4).
- To make the cookies: Make Fantastic Fairy Cookies dough according to directions. Use a large ice cream/cookie scoop or pinch off dough and roll into a golf ball–size ball; place about 4 or 5 cookie balls on a greased baking sheet. Flatten slightly and insert a stick into each flattened cookie.
- Bake for about 15 to 20 minutes, or until cookies are golden around the edges and firm in the center. Let sit for 2 minutes on baking sheet, then remove with a spatula and place on a flat surface to cool completely.
- To make the frosting: Combine all frosting ingredients in a food processor and blend until smooth. Frost each cooled cookie pop. Decorate with desired toppings.
- For a fun gift, wrap the cookies in cellophane or colored plastic wrap. Tie ribbon around the stick at the base of the cookie.

Yield: 18 cookie pops

Fantastic Fairy Cookies

What wee one wouldn't want a frosted Fantastic Fairy cookie? Have them help you decorate these dainty little cookies. Calling a food something fun is a good trick for those picky eaters who will not try anything new. This makes the best cut-out cookie dough! This dough has a great sugar cookie flavor.

FOR COOKIES

½ cup (125 g) unsweetened
   applesauce

½ cup (60 g) powdered sugar
   (contains cornstarch; can use corn-
   free recipe on page 43)

½ cup (100 g) superfine sugar

2 teaspoons (10 ml) vanilla extract

½ cup (100 g) Spectrum
   Organic Shortening

¼ teaspoon (1.5 g) salt

½ teaspoon (2.3 g) baking soda

½ teaspoon (2.3 g) cream of tartar

1 ½ cups (185 g) Bob's Red Mill
   white rice flour

1 cup (125 g) Bob's Red Mill
   tapioca flour

FOR FROSTING

¼ cup (50 g) Spectrum
   Organic Shortening

1 teaspoon (5 ml) vanilla extract

2 cups (240 g) powdered sugar
   (contains cornstarch; can use corn-
   free recipe on page 43)

1 tablespoon (15 ml) water

Dash of salt

FOR TOPPING

¼ cup (40 g) "safe" candy pieces,
   peppermints, sulfite-free dried
   fruit, or colored sugars

DIRECTIONS

- Preheat oven to 350°F (180°C, or gas mark 4).
- To make the cookies: Cream together applesauce, sugars, vanilla, shortening, and salt. Add the remaining cookie ingredients, start the mixer slow and work up to medium speed. Mix until batter is smooth.
- Pinch off 1 to 2 teaspoons (5 to 10 g) of dough and roll into balls. Place on a baking sheet and flatten slightly. Or, to make decorated cookie shapes with cookie cutters, divide dough into fourths. Place one section of dough between two pieces of nonstick parchment paper. With a rolling pin, roll dough into a flat ½-inch (1.2-cm) disc. Using a cookie cutter, press firmly into dough and with a flat spatula gently remove the cookie shapes to a greased baking sheet. Collect remaining scrap dough and repeat process.
- Bake for about 12 to 15 minutes, or until the cookies are darker around the edges and firm in the centers. Watch the cookies to make sure they don't get too golden. Remove from baking sheet with a flat spatula and place on a flat surface to cool.
- To make the frosting: Place frosting ingredients in a food processor and process until smooth. Place in a bowl.
- To make the topping: Place candies in a resealable plastic bag and crush with a rolling pin. Pour candy pieces in a small bowl.
- Decorate cooled cookies with frosting and sprinkle with candy pieces or colored sugar if desired.

Yield: About 3 dozen

Choco Cherry Chunk Cookies

This is one of my favorite combinations in a cookie: dark chocolate chunks, sweet dried cherries, and a delicious caramel flavor. You will find yourself making these often!

⅓ cup (80 ml) vegetable oil

1 cup (225 g) packed brown sugar

1 teaspoon (5 ml) vanilla extract

¼ teaspoon (1.5 g) salt

1¼ cups (125 g) certified gluten-free oat bran or oats, ground into a oat bran consistency

½ cup (60 g) Bob's Red Mill white rice flour

1 teaspoon (4.6 g) baking powder

¼ cup (60 ml) water

3 (1.4-ounce, or 40-g) Enjoy Life boom CHOCO boom dark chocolate bars, chopped into 1-inch (2.5-cm) chunks

1 cup (145 g) sulfite-free dried cherries

DIRECTIONS

- Preheat oven to 350°F (180°C, or gas mark 4).
- In a bowl, mix together oil, brown sugar, vanilla, and salt. Add oat bran, flour, and baking powder and mix. While mixing, slowly pour in the water until the dough is smooth. Stir in the chocolate chunks and cherries.
- Use a small ice cream/cookie scoop or drop dough by tablespoon onto a baking sheet, spacing the cookies about 4 inches (10 cm) apart (about 6 cookies per baking sheet). Cookies will spread as they bake.
- Bake for about 12 to 15 minutes, or until golden around the edges and soft in the center. Let cool on baking sheet for less than 10 minutes. Remove with a spatula and place on a flat surface to cool completely.

Yield: About 2 dozen

Orange These Delicious? Cookies

FOR COOKIES

1/4 cup (60 ml) orange juice
   concentrate

1/4 cup (60 ml) water

1/2 cup (60 g) powdered sugar
   (contains cornstarch; can use corn-
   free recipe on page 43)

1/2 cup (100 g) superfine sugar

2 teaspoons (10 ml) vanilla extract

1/2 cup (100 g) Spectrum
   Organic Shortening

1/4 teaspoon (1.5 g) salt

1 teaspoon (1.7 g) orange zest

1/2 teaspoon (2.3 g) baking soda

1/2 teaspoon (2.3 g) cream of tartar

1 1/2 cups (185 g) Bob's Red Mill white
   rice flour

1 cup (125 g) Bob's Red Mill
   tapioca flour

FOR VANILLA ORANGE FROSTING

1 cup (120 g) powdered sugar
   (contains cornstarch; can use corn-
   free recipe on page 43)

1 teaspoon (5 ml) vanilla extract

1 tablespoon (15 ml) orange juice

FOR CHOCOLATE FROSTING

2 cups (240 g) powdered sugar
   (contains cornstarch; can use corn-
   free recipe on page 43)

1/3 cup (29 g) unsweetened
   cocoa powder

1/3 cup (67 g) Spectrum
   Organic Shortening

2 teaspoons (10 ml) vanilla extract

3 to 4 tablespoons (45 to 60 ml)
   water

DIRECTIONS

- Preheat oven to 350°F (180°C, or gas mark 4).
- To make the cookies: Cream together orange juice, water, sugars, vanilla, shortening, salt, and zest. Add the remaining cookie ingredients, start the mixer slow, and work up to medium speed. Mix until batter is smooth.
- Pinch off 1 to 2 teaspoons (5 to 10 g) of dough and roll into balls. Place on a baking sheet. Flatten slightly.
- Bake for about 12 to 15 minutes. Remove with a spatula and cool.
- To make the frostings: Place each kind of frosting ingredients in a separate, clean food processor and process until smooth. Frost each cookie.

Yield: About 3 dozen

Fudge Top Vanilla Drops

FOR COOKIES

½ cup (125 g) unsweetened
   applesauce

½ cup (60 g) powdered sugar
   (contains cornstarch; can use corn-
   free recipe on page 43)

½ cup (100 g) superfine sugar

2 teaspoon (10 ml) vanilla extract

½ cup (100 g) Spectrum
   Organic Shortening

¼ teaspoon (1.5 g) salt

½ teaspoon (2.3 g) baking soda

½ teaspoon (2.3 g) cream of tartar

1 ½ cups (185 g) Bob's Red Mill
   white rice flour

1 cup (125 g) Bob's Red Mill
   tapioca flour

FOR FUDGE FROSTING

¼ cup (50 g) Spectrum
   Organic Shortening

3 tablespoons (45 ml) water

2 cups (240 g) powdered sugar
   (contains cornstarch; can use corn-
   free recipe on page 43)

2 tablespoons (11 g) unsweetened
   cocoa powder

Dash of salt

DIRECTIONS

- Preheat oven to 350°F (180°C, or gas mark 4).
- To make the cookies: Cream together applesauce, sugars, vanilla, shortening, and salt. Add the remaining cookie ingredients, start the mixer slow, and work up to medium speed. Mix until batter is smooth.
- Pinch off 1 to 2 teaspoons (5 to 10 g) of dough and roll into balls, or use a small ice cream/cookie scoop and drop dough onto a baking sheet. Flatten slightly.
- Bake for about 12 to 15 minutes. Remove from baking sheet and cool.
- To make the frosting: Combine all ingredients in a food processor until smooth. Frost each cooled cookie.

Yield: About 3 dozen

Oatmeal Choco Chunk-a-Hunk Drops

1 cup (245 g) unsweetened
  applesauce
1 ¹/₂ cups (345 g) packed brown sugar
¹/₄ cup (60 ml) vegetable oil
¹/₄ cup (60 ml) water
3 cups (240 g) certified gluten-free
  rolled oats
1 cup (125 g) Bob's Red Mill white or
  brown rice flour

¹/₂ cup (60 g) Bob's Red Mill
  tapioca flour
¹/₄ teaspoon (1.5 g) salt
3 (1.4-ounce, or 40-g) Enjoy Life
  boom CHOCO boom dark chocolate or dairy-free rice milk bars, cut
  into 1-inch (2.5-cm) chunks

DIRECTIONS

- Preheat oven to 375°F (190°C, or gas mark 5).
- In a saucepan, stir together the applesauce, brown sugar, oil, and water. Cook over medium heat until melted, stirring occasionally. Remove from heat. Add in oats, flours, and salt. Stir in chocolate chunks.
- Drop batter by rounded tablespoons onto a baking sheet.
- Bake for 10 minutes or until edges are firm. Cool on baking sheet for 2 minutes. Remove to a flat surface to cool completely.

Yield: About 3 dozen

Outrageous Oatmeal Cookies

This wholesome, filling cookie is great for on the go.

1 cup (340 g) honey or (235 ml) pure maple syrup

1/2 cup (120 ml) vegetable oil

1/2 cup (125 g) unsweetened applesauce

1 teaspoon (5 ml) vanilla extract

1 cup (125 g) Bob's Red Mill brown or white rice flour

1/2 cup (60 g) Bob's Red Mill tapioca flour

2 1/2 cups (200 g) certified gluten-free rolled oats

1 teaspoon (2.3 g) ground cinnamon

1/2 teaspoon (2.3 g) baking soda

Dash of salt

1 1/2 cups (225 g) Enjoy Life Not Nuts! trail mix of your choice

DIRECTIONS

- Preheat oven to 350°F (180°C, or gas mark 4).
- With a mixer, cream together honey, oil, applesauce, and vanilla. Add in rice flour and next 5 ingredients (through salt) and mix until well combined. Stir in trail mix.
- Drop dough by rounded tablespoon onto a greased baking sheet.
- Bake for 15 minutes. Let sit on baking sheet for 2 minutes, then remove to a flat surface to cool completely.

Yield: About 4 dozen

Caramel-icious Chocolate Lace Cookies

*I love the flavor of "caramel" and the giant chocolate chunks
in this delicious lacy cookie.*

⅓ cup (80 ml) vegetable oil

1 cup (225 g) packed brown sugar

1 teaspoon (5 ml) vanilla extract

¼ teaspoon (1.5 g) salt

1 ¼ cups (125 g) certified gluten-free
  oat bran

½ cup (60 g) Bob's Red Mill white
  rice flour"

1 teaspoon (4.6 g) baking powder

¼ cup (60 ml) water

3 (1.4-ounce, or 40-g) Enjoy Life
  boom CHOCO boom dark chocolate bars, chopped into 1-inch
  (2.5-cm) chunks

DIRECTIONS

- Preheat oven to 350°F (180°C, or gas mark 4).

- In a bowl, mix together oil, brown sugar, vanilla, and salt. Add oat bran, flour, and baking powder and mix. While mixing, slowly pour in the water until the dough is smooth. Stir in the chocolate chunks.

- Use a small ice cream/cookie scoop or drop dough by tablespoon onto a baking sheet, spacing the cookies about 4 inches (10 cm) apart (about 6 cookies per baking sheet). Cookies will spread as they bake.

- Bake for about 12 to 15 minutes, or until golden around the edges and soft in the center. Let cool on baking sheet for less than 10 minutes. Remove with a spatula and place on a flat surface to cool completely.

Yield: About 4 dozen

Chapter 6

Bar Cookies

Bar cookies are convenient to make. This chapter offers many varieties from fruity snack bars to decadent chocolaty treats. You can jazz up the bars with frostings and chocolate drizzles, or leave them plain. Whichever bar you choose, I am sure you will enjoy!

Frost on the Pumpk'n Bars

These bar cookies are a delicious treat in the morning. My kids
like that they taste like iced pumpkin pie.

FOR BARS

1 cup (245 g) canned pumpkin

½ cup (120 ml) vegetable oil

1 teaspoon (5 ml) vanilla extract

½ cup (115 g) firmly packed light
   brown sugar

1 cup (125 g) Bob's Red Mill white rice
   flour (or ½ cup [60 g] rice flour and
   ½ cup [60 g] oat or sorghum flour)

1 teaspoon (4.6 g) baking powder

2 teaspoons (4.6 g) ground cinnamon
   or pumpkin pie spice (see 42)

¼ teaspoon (1.5 g) salt

FOR ICING

¼ cup (50 g) Spectrum
   Organic Shortening

1 cup (120 g) powdered sugar
   (contains cornstarch; can use
   corn-free recipe on page 43)

1 tablespoon (15 ml) rice milk, safe
   milk alternative, or water

1 teaspoon (5 ml) vanilla extract

Dash of salt

DIRECTIONS

- Preheat oven to 350°F (180°C, or gas mark 4).
- To make the bars: With a mixer, beat the pumpkin, oil, vanilla, and brown sugar
  until smooth. Add the remaining bar ingredients and mix until well combined.
  Pour into a greased 9-inch (23-cm) square baking pan.
- Bake for 25 to 30 minutes or until bars are golden brown around the edges and
  firm in the center. Let cool.
- To make the icing: Combine all icing ingredients in a food processor and blend
  together until smooth with no lumps.
- Pour icing over the cooled pumpkin bars and spread evenly; cut into bars. Or, cut
  into bars and then drizzle the icing in zigzags over the tops. Place in the refrigerator
  to let icing set.

Yield: About 2 dozen

Choco-Top Brownies

These brownies are super-sweet and chocolaty!

FOR BROWNIES

½ cup (125 g) unsweetened
   applesauce

⅓ cup (80 ml) water

⅓ cup (80 ml) vegetable oil

1 tablespoon (15 ml) vanilla extract

¾ cup (65 g) unsweetened
   cocoa powder

1 cup (200 g) superfine sugar

1 ⅓ cups (165 g) Bob's Red Mill
   white rice flour

¼ teaspoon (1.5 g) salt

1 teaspoon (4.6 g) baking powder

FOR FROSTING

2 cups (240 g) powdered sugar
   (contains cornstarch; can use
   corn-free recipe on page 43)

⅔ cup (57 g) unsweetened
   cocoa powder

½ cup (100 g) Spectrum
   Organic Shortening

1 tablespoon (15 ml) vanilla extract

¼ cup (60 ml) rice milk, or safe
   milk alternative, or water

FOR TOPPING

1 (1.4-ounce, or 40-g) Enjoy Life
   boom CHOCO boom dark chocolate
   or dairy-free rice milk bar, chopped
   into small chunks

DIRECTIONS

- Preheat oven to 350°F (180°C, or gas mark 4).
- To make the brownies: With a mixer, beat the applesauce, water, oil, vanilla, cocoa, and sugar until smooth. Add the flour, salt, and baking powder and mix until well combined. Pour into a greased 9-inch (23-cm) square baking pan.
- Bake for 25 to 30 minutes or until firm around the corners and an indentation remains when you poke it in the middle with your finger. Let cool completely.
- To make the frosting: Combine frosting ingredients and mix until smooth. Add additional rice milk to achieve desired consistency. Spread over cooled brownie in pan.
- Sprinkle chopped chocolate bar over frosting. Refrigerate for about 30 minutes. Cut into bars or squares.

Yield: About 2 dozen

Banana-danna Streusel Bars

Use firm, ripe (not brown or green but yellow) bananas for this cookie treat.
It has a cookie crust, a luscious creamy banana center, and a streusel top.
These are great served warm.

FOR CRUST

½ cup (115 g) packed brown sugar

½ cup (60 g) Bob's Red Mill
tapioca flour

1 cup (125 g) Bob's Red Mill white or
brown rice or sorghum flour

½ teaspoon (1.2 g) ground cinnamon

½ teaspoon (2.3 g) baking powder

Dash of salt

¼ cup (60 ml) vegetable oil

¼ cup (60 ml) water

FOR FILLING

5 ripe medium bananas, sliced

¼ cup (50 g) superfine sugar

½ teaspoon (1.2 g) ground cinnamon

1 cup (235 ml) unsweetened
pineapple juice

¼ cup (60 ml) water

3 tablespoons (24 g) cornstarch
(contains corn; can use tapioca or
arrowroot starch instead)

FOR STREUSEL TOPPING

¼ cup (30 g) Bob's Red Mill
tapioca flour

¼ cup (30 g) Bob's Red Mill brown
or white rice or sorghum flour

½ cup (115 g) packed brown sugar

½ teaspoon (1.2 g) ground cinnamon

1 tablespoon (15 ml) vegetable oil

1 tablespoon (15 ml) water

DIRECTIONS

- Preheat oven to 350°F (180°C, or gas mark 4).
- To make the crust: Place all crust ingredients in a food processor. Blend until dough forms into a ball. Press dough into a greased 9 x 13-inch (23 x 33-cm) baking pan.
- To make the filling: Toss the banana slices with the sugar and cinnamon. Spoon bananas onto cookie crust.
- In a saucepan whisk together the pineapple juice, water, and starch. Cook over medium heat until bubbly, stirring occasionally. Pour over banana mixture.
- To make the streusel topping: Place topping ingredients in a food processor and pulse until mixture resembles crumbs. Sprinkle over top of banana mixture.
- Cover pan with aluminum foil. Bake for about 40 minutes. Let cool slightly and cut into bars while warm.

Yield: About 2 dozen

DID YOU KNOW?
Food allergies affect children and adults of all races and ethnicity, and can develop at any age.
(Source: Food Allergy Initiative)

Bran' New Day Bars

¼ cup (60 g) packed brown sugar

1 cup (235 ml) rice milk, safe milk alternative, or apple juice

¼ cup (85 g) honey

¼ cup (60 ml) vegetable oil

Dash of salt

1 cup (125 g) Bob's Red Mill brown rice flour

1 cup (100 g) rice bran

½ cup (56 g) flax meal

1 tablespoon (14 g) baking powder

1 teaspoon (2.3 g) ground cinnamon

1 cup (165 g) packed sulfite-free raisins, chopped dates, or dried cranberries

DIRECTIONS

- Preheat oven to 350°F (180°C, or gas mark 4).
- Stir together the brown sugar, rice milk, honey, oil, and salt. Add the flour and next 4 ingredients (through cinnamon). Stir together for about 30 seconds. Stir in the raisins.
- Pour into a greased 9 x 13-inch (23 x 33-cm) baking pan.
- Bake for about 25 minutes, or until firm in the center. Let cool. Cut into bars or squares.

Yield: About 2 dozen

Oh-Oh Oh-range Pumpkin Bars

FOR BARS

1 cup (225 g) packed brown sugar

²/₃ cup (160 ml) orange juice or water

1 cup (245 g) canned pumpkin

¹/₄ cup (60 ml) vegetable oil

1 teaspoon (5 ml) vanilla extract

¹/₄ teaspoon (1.5 g) salt

2 cups (250 g) Bob's Red Mill white or brown rice flour

2 teaspoons (9. 2 g) baking powder

¹/₂ teaspoon (2.3 g) baking soda

1 cup (120 g) finely shredded carrots

1 teaspoon (1.7 g) orange zest

¹/₂ cup (83 g) packed golden sulfite free raisins (optional)

FOR ICING (OPTIONAL)

¹/₂ cup (60 g) powdered sugar (contains cornstarch; can use corn-free recipe on page 43)

2 tablespoons (30 ml) orange juice

DIRECTIONS

- Preheat oven to 350°F (180°C, or gas mark 4).
- To make the bars: Cream together the brown sugar, orange juice, pumpkin, oil, vanilla, and salt. Add flour, baking powder, and baking soda and mix until well combined. Stir in carrots, orange zest, and raisins.
- Pour batter into a greased 9 x 13-inch (23 x 33-cm) baking pan. Bake for 25 to 30 minutes or until firm in the center. Let cool.
- To make the icing, if using: Combine powdered sugar and orange juice in a bowl and stir until smooth.
- Spread icing over cooled cake. Cut into bars. Sprinkle with orange zest if desired.

Yield: About 2 dozen

The Best "Shortbread"

Cornstarch is the secret to the tender melt-in-your-mouth texture. You may use the tapioca starch or arrowroot starch, but the shortbread comes out a bit tougher. This is truly a delicious cookie. If you want to impress someone with your allergy-friendly baking, make these.

½ cup (100 g) Spectrum Organic Shortening

½ cup (60 g) Bob's Red Mill white rice flour

½ cup (65 g) cornstarch (contains corn; can use tapioca or arrowroot starch instead)

½ cup (60 g) powdered sugar (contains cornstarch; can use corn-free recipe on page 43)

⅛ teaspoon (0.6 g) baking powder

⅛ teaspoon (0.8 g) salt

1 teaspoon (5 ml) vanilla

DIRECTIONS

- Preheat oven to 350°F (180°C, or gas mark 4).
- In a food processor, combine all ingredients and process for 1 minute. It will look very crumbly for the first few moments but should form into a ball. Once the dough comes together, remove from the food processor and use your hands to form the dough into a ball. Place on a greased baking sheet and shape into an even circle. Pinch the edges and use a sharp knife to cut into 8 slices. Do not separate the slices.
- Bake for about 17 minutes, or until edges are golden; the centers should remain white, not browned. Let sit for half an hour on baking sheet to cool. With a sharp knife, re-cut along the edges of each slice. Sprinkle with powdered sugar, if desired.

Yield: 8 wedges

RECIPE NOTE
Recipe does not work well with blended flour mix.

Date to Remember Bars

One of my tasters' favorite recipes.

FOR COOKIE BASE

1/2 cup (100 g) Spectrum
   Organic Shortening

1 cup (225 g) packed brown sugar

1 cup (125 g) Bob's Red Mill white or
   brown rice flour or sorghum flour

1/2 teaspoon (3 g) salt

3/4 cup (94 g) Bob's Red Mill
   tapioca flour

1 1/2 cups (120 g) certified gluten-free
   rolled oats

FOR FILLING

3 cups (500 g) sulfite-free dates,
   cut into small pieces

1/4 cup (50 g) superfine sugar

1 1/2 cups (355 ml) water

DIRECTIONS

- Preheat oven to 350°F (180°C, or gas mark 4).
- To make the cookie base: In a food processor, combine the cookie base ingredients and pulse until it resembles crumbs. Press half the mixture into a greased 9 x 13-inch (23 x 33-cm) baking pan. Set the other half of the mixture aside.
- To make the filling: Place the dates, sugar, and water in a saucepan. Cook over low heat until thickened (about 10 minutes), stirring constantly. Cool.
- Spread date mixture on cookie base crust in pan. Sprinkle reserved crumb mixture evenly over the date filling.
- Bake for 35 to 40 minutes, or until lightly browned. Let cool slightly. While still warm, cut into bars and remove from pan.

Yield: About 3 dozen

Cocoa-Carrot Carumba Bars

FOR BARS

½ cup (125 g) unsweetened
 applesauce

⅓ cup (29 g) unsweetened
 cocoa powder

⅔ cup (135 g) superfine sugar

¼ cup (60 ml) vegetable oil

Dash of salt

1 cup (125 g) Bob's Red Mill white
 rice flour

¼ cup (30 g) Bob's Red Mill
 tapioca flour

2 teaspoons (9.2 g) baking powder

1 cup (120 g) finely shredded carrots

FOR FROSTING

2 cups (240 g) powdered sugar
 (contains cornstarch; can use
 corn-free recipe on page 43)

⅓ cup (29 g) unsweetened
 cocoa powder

⅓ cup (67 g) Spectrum
 Organic Shortening

2 teaspoons (10 ml) vanilla extract

3 to 4 tablespoons (45 to 60 ml)
 water

DIRECTIONS

- Preheat oven to 350°F (180°C, or gas mark 4).
- To make the bars: Cream together the applesauce, cocoa, sugar, oil, and salt. Add flours and baking powder and blend until smooth. Stir in shredded carrots.
- Pour into a greased 9 x 13-inch (23 x 33-cm) baking pan.
- Bake for about 50 minutes. Let cool.
- To make the frosting: Mix all frosting ingredients until smooth. Use to frost cooled cake. Cut into bars.

Yield: About 2 dozen

Carrot Banana Bonanza Cakes

FOR BARS

¼ cup (60 ml) vegetable oil

¼ cup (60 ml) rice milk, safe milk
   alternative, or water

¾ cup (170 g) packed brown sugar

2 bananas, sliced

1 cup (125 g) Bob's Red Mill white
   rice flour

1 teaspoon (4.6 g) baking powder

½ teaspoon (2.3 g) baking soda

1 teaspoon (2.3 g) ground cinnamon

Dash of salt

½ cup (60 g) finely grated carrots

2 tablespoons (18 g) sunflower
   seeds kernels

¼ cup (40 g) sulfite-free raisins

FOR FROSTING

½ cup (60 g) powdered sugar
   (contains cornstarch; can use
   corn-free recipe on page 43)

½ teaspoon (1.2 g) ground cinnamon

1 to 2 teaspoons (5 to 10 ml) rice milk,
   safe milk alternative, or water

DIRECTIONS

- Preheat oven to 350°F (180°C, or gas mark 4).
- To make the bars: In a food processor, combine the oil, milk, brown sugar, and bananas and blend until smooth. Add the flour and the next 4 ingredients (through salt) and pulse until well combined. Stir in the shredded carrots. After the carrots are well incorporated, stir in the sunflower seeds and raisins.
- Pour batter into a greased 8-inch (20-cm) square pan.
- Bake for about 25 minutes, or until cake feels firm to the touch in the center. Let cool completely.
- To make the frosting: Cream together all the frosting ingredients. Add additional rice milk until you reach the desired consistency.
- Drizzle the frosting over the cake in the pan and then cut out into bars. Sprinkle additional cinnamon on top, if desired.

Yield: 16 bars

Berry Good Apricot Bars

½ cup (125 g) unsweetened applesauce

⅓ cup (67 g) superfine sugar, plus additional for topping

Dash of salt

2 cups (250 g) Bob's Red Mill white rice flour

¼ cup (30 g) Bob's Red Mill tapioca flour

2 teaspoons (9.2 g) baking powder

⅔ cup (160 ml) apple juice

1 cup (110 g) fresh raspberries

½ cup (80 g) dried sulfite-free apricots, cut into tiny pieces

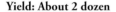

DIRECTIONS

- Preheat oven to 350°F (180°C, or gas mark 4).
- With a mixer,, combine together the applesauce, sugar, and salt. Add the flours and baking powder and mix until well combined. With the mixer on low speed, slowly pour in the apple juice until you have a smooth dough. Gently stir in the raspberries and apricot pieces.
- Pour batter into a greased 9-inch (23-cm) baking pan. Sprinkle with additional sugar, if desired.
- Bake for about 45 minutes, or until golden around the edges. Cool completely before cutting into bars. Dust heavily with superfine sugar (or powdered sugar), if desired, and additional fresh raspberries

Yield: About 2 dozen

Fresh Take Fruitcake Bars

These are made in a slightly unusual way, but the result is a moist and rich cookie bar.

1 ½ cups (355 ml) water

1 cup (120 g) grated carrots

1 cup (165 g) packed sulfite-free
   raisins or chopped prunes

¾ cup (255 g) honey

2 tablespoons (30 ml) vegetable oil

1 teaspoon (2.3 g) ground cinnamon

1 teaspoon (6 g) salt

½ teaspoon (1.1 g) ground nutmeg

¼ teaspoon (0.5 g) ground cloves

1 cup (125 g) Bob's Red Mill brown
   rice or sorghum flour

½ cup (60 g) Bob's Red Mill
   tapioca flour

1 teaspoon (4.6 g) baking soda

½ cup (50 g) rice bran

½ cup (56 g) flax meal

1 cup (150 g) Enjoy Life Not Nuts!
  Mountain Mambo trail mix

DIRECTIONS

- Preheat oven to 350°F (180°C, or gas mark 4).
- In a saucepan, combine water, carrots, raisins, honey, oil, cinnamon, salt, nutmeg, and cloves. Cook over medium-low heat for about 10 minutes, or until carrots are soft. Let cool slightly.
- In a large bowl, combine flours, baking soda, rice bran, and flax. Add carrot mixture to flour mixture and stir until well combined. Stir in trail mix.
- Pour batter into a greased 9 x 13-inch (23 x 33-cm) baking pan.
- Bake for about 30 minutes, or until firm in the center. Let cool and cut into bars.

Yield: About 2 dozen

Apple Ginger Spice Bars

*This is a great treat at anytime. Not too sweet tasting and a little spicy.
The apple pieces make a moist and delicious addition.*

⅓ cup (80 ml) plus 1 tablespoon
 (15 ml) vegetable oil

1 cup (225 g) packed brown sugar

2 tablespoons (40 g) unsulfured
 molasses

2 cups (250 g) Bob's Red Mill brown
 rice flour

1 teaspoon (4.6 g) baking powder

1 tablespoon (13.8 g) baking soda

2 ½ teaspoons (4.5 g) ground ginger

¾ cup (180 ml) apple juice

2 medium apples, chopped into
 small pieces

DIRECTIONS

- Preheat oven to 350°F (180°C, or gas mark 4).
- Mix the oil, brown sugar, and molasses. Add the flour and next 3 ingredients
  (through ginger) and mix to combine. With mixer on low, slowly add the apple
  juice. The dough should be smooth, like cake dough. Stir in the apple pieces.
- Bake for 40 minutes or until golden around the edges. Cool completely and cut
  into squares.

Yield: About 2 dozen

Chompin' Choco Chip Banana Bars

Light and tasty. If you like banana bread, you will enjoy these.

¼ cup (60 ml) vegetable oil

¼ cup (60 ml) rice milk, safe milk alternative, or water

⅔ cup (135 g) superfine sugar

1 tablespoon (15 ml) vanilla extract

3 ripe bananas, sliced

1 ½ cups (185 g) Bob's Red Mill white rice flour

½ cup (60 g) Bob's Red Mill tapioca flour

2 teaspoons (9.2 g) baking powder

1 cup (175 g) Enjoy Life semi-sweet chocolate chips

DIRECTIONS

- Preheat oven to 350°F (180°C, or gas mark 4).
- In a food processor purée the oil, milk, sugar, vanilla, and bananas until smooth. Add the flours and baking powder and pulse until the dough is smooth. Stir in the chocolate chips.
- Pour batter into a greased 9 x 13-inch (23 x 33-cm) pan.
- Bake for about 30 minutes, or until golden around the edges and soft in the center. Let cool in the pan. Top with additional chocolate chips if desired. Cut into bars or squares.

Yield: About 2 dozen

M-M-Molasses Multigrain Bars

This reminds me of Boston Brown Bread.

1/3 cup (80 ml) unsulfured molasses

1 tablespoon (15 ml) vegetable oil

1/4 cup (60 g) packed brown sugar

1/4 teaspoon (1.5 g) salt

1/2 cup (60 g) Bob's Red Mill
  millet flour

1/2 cup (60 g) Bob's Red Mill
  sorghum flour

1/2 cup (56 g) flax meal

1 cup (235 ml) rice milk or safe
  milk alternative

1 teaspoon (5 ml) white vinegar

1 cup (165 g) packed sulfite-free
  raisins

DIRECTIONS

- Preheat oven to 350°F (180°C, or gas mark 4).

- Mix together molasses, oil, brown sugar, and salt. Add in the flours and flax meal. Set aside.

- In a bowl, combine the rice milk and vinegar. With mixer on low, slowly add the rice milk mixture to the molasses mixture. Blend until well combined. Stir in the raisins.

- Spoon batter into a 9 x 13-inch greased (23 x 33-cm) baking pan and cover with aluminum foil.

- Bake for about 35 minutes, or until firm to the touch. Remove aluminum foil and let cool. Cut into squares. Serve warm.

Yield: About 2 dozen

Lemon-licious Shortbread

This is a very delicate and delicious cookie. The lemon icing makes for a fancy touch.

FOR SHORTBREAD

½ cup (100 g) Spectrum Organic Shortening

¾ cup (94 g) Bob's Red Mill white rice flour

½ cup (65 g) cornstarch (contains corn; can use arrowroot starch)

½ cup (50 g) powdered sugar (contains cornstarch; can use corn-free recipe on page 43)

⅛ teaspoon (0.6 g) baking powder

⅛ teaspoon (0.8 g) salt

1 tablespoon (15 ml) lemon juice

1 teaspoon (1.7 g) lemon zest

FOR ICING

1 cup (120g) powdered sugar (or use corn-free recipe on page 43)

2 teaspoons (10 ml) lemon juice

2 teaspoons (3.4 g) lemon zest

DIRECTIONS

- Preheat oven to 350°F (180°C, or gas mark 4).
- To make the shortbread: In a food processor, combine all shortbread ingredients and process for 1 minute. Using your hands, press dough into an 8-inch (20-cm) square baking pan lined with aluminum foil.
- Bake for about 25 minutes, or until edges are golden. Let sit for half an hour on a baking sheet to cool. With a sharp knife, cut into small bars. Carefully remove from pan with a small spatula.
- To make the icing: Mix together the powdered sugar and lemon juice. With a spoon, drizzle icing over each bar. Sprinkle a touch of lemon zest over each iced bar if desired. Let icing harden before serving.

Yield: 12 bars

RECIPE NOTE

Recipe does not work well with blended flour mix.

Pear Crisp Crunchy Bars

FOR CRUST

½ cup (115 g) packed brown sugar

½ cup (60 g) Bob's Red Mill
   tapioca flour

1 cup (125 g) Bob's Red Mill brown
   rice or sorghum flour

½ teaspoon (1.2 g) ground cinnamon

½ teaspoon (2.3 g) baking powder

Dash of salt

¼ cup (60 ml) vegetable oil

¼ cup (60 ml) water

FOR FILLING

6 firm pears, red or green

½ cup (125 g) unsweetened
   applesauce

¼ cup (60 g) packed brown sugar

1 teaspoon (2.3 g) ground cinnamon

1 tablespoon (8 g) cornstarch
   (contains corn; can use tapioca or
   arrowroot starch instead)

FOR TOPPING

¾ cup (60 g) certified gluten-
   free oats

3 tablespoons (21 g) flax meal

3 tablespoons (45 g) packed
   brown sugar

1 teaspoon (2.3 g) ground cinnamon

2 tablespoons (30 ml) vegetable oil

1 tablespoon (15 ml) water

DIRECTIONS

- Preheat oven to 350°F (180°C, or gas mark 4).
- To make the crust: Combine all crust ingredients in a food processor and pulse until dough forms into a ball. Press dough into a greased 9 x 13-inch (23 x 33-cm) baking pan.
- To make the filling: Chop the pears into small pieces and stir in remaining filling ingredients. Pour over crust.
- To make the topping: Place all topping ingredients in a food processor and pulse a few times until mixture resembles crumbs. Sprinkle over filling.
- Bake for about 40 minutes. Cool completely and cut into bars.

Yield: About 2 dozen

Bodacious Blondie Swirl Bars

These are like a cake bar swirled with chocolate and packed with chocolate chips. Yum! I love these.

¼ cup (50 g) Spectrum Organic Shortening

1 ½ cups (345 g) plus 1 tablespoon (15 g) packed brown sugar, divided

⅓ cup (80 ml) plus 1 tablespoon (15 ml) water, divided

½ cup (125 g) unsweetened applesauce

2 teaspoons (10 ml) vanilla extract

½ teaspoon (3 g) salt

2 cups (250 g) Bob's Red Mill white rice flour

¼ cup (30 g) Bob's Red Mill tapioca flour

2 ½ teaspoons (11.5 g) baking powder

⅔ cup (117 g) Enjoy Life semi-sweet chocolate chips

1 tablespoon (5.4 g) unsweetened cocoa powder

DIRECTIONS

- Preheat oven to 350°F (180°C, or gas mark 4).
- In a medium saucepan, combine shortening, 1½ cups (345 g) brown sugar, ⅓ cup (80 ml) water, and applesauce. Cook over low heat until smooth, about 1 minute. Remove from heat and stir in vanilla and next 4 ingredients (through baking powder) with a wooden spoon. Stir until batter is smooth.
- Quickly stir in chocolate chips and spread into a greased 9 x 13-inch (23 x 33-cm) baking pan.
- Combine cocoa, remaining 1 tablespoon (15 g) brown sugar, and remaining 1 tablespoon (15 ml) water and stir until you have a paste. Drop chocolate mixture by teaspoonfuls around the pan. Run a knife through the batter to create a swirl pattern.
- Bake for about 25 minutes, or until sides are golden and center is soft to the touch. Cool completely. Cut into bars.

Yield: About 2 dozen

Berry-Berry Orange Iced Bars

A flavorful and moist snack bar. You may serve with or without the icing.

FOR BARS

1 ½ cups (355 ml) orange juice
  (or 1 cup [235 ml] water and
  ½ cup [120 ml] orange juice
  concentrate)

1 cup (200 g) sugar

¼ cup (60 ml) vegetable oil

1 teaspoon (5 ml) vanilla

3 cups (375 g) Bob's Red Mill
  white rice flour

1 tablespoon (13.8 g) baking powder

½ teaspoon (3 g) salt

1 ½ cups (218 g) fresh or frozen
  blueberries

FOR ICING (OPTIONAL)

1 cup (120 g) powdered sugar
  (contains cornstarch; can use
  corn-free recipe on page 43)

2 teaspoons (10 ml) orange juice

DIRECTIONS

- Preheat oven to 350°F (180°C, or gas mark 4).
- To make the bars: In a large bowl, combine orange juice and next 6 ingredients (through salt) and mix until smooth. Stir in blueberries.
- Pour batter into a greased 9 x 13-inch (23 x 33-cm) baking pan.
- Bake for about 40 minutes, or until the center cracks. Let cool.
- To make the icing: Stir together the powdered sugar and orange juice. Pour icing over cooled cake. Cut into bars. Sprinkle with lemon zest if desired.

Yield: About 2 dozen

Chocolate Chip Cookie Bark

½ cup (100 g) Spectrum Organic Shortening

½ cup (60 g) Bob's Red Mill white rice flour

½ cup (65 g) cornstarch (contains corn; can use tapioca or arrowroot starch instead)

½ cup (60 g) powdered sugar (contains cornstarch; can use corn-free recipe on page 43)

⅛ teaspoon (0.6 g) baking powder

⅛ teaspoon (0.8 g) salt

1 teaspoon (5 ml) vanilla

1 cup (175 g) Enjoy Life semi-sweet chocolate chips

1 (1.4-ounce, or 40-g) Enjoy Life boom CHOCO boom dark chocolate or dairy-free rice milk bar

DIRECTIONS

- Preheat oven to 350°F (180°C, or gas mark 4).

- In a food processor, combine shortening and next 6 ingredients (through vanilla) and process for 1 minute, or until dough starts to come together. Add in chocolate chips and pulse a few times.

- Spread into a greased 9 x 13-inch (23 x 33-cm) baking pan.

- Bake for about 17 minutes, or until edges are golden. Set aside.

- Break chocolate bar into small pieces. Place in a microwave-proof bowl and heat at 30-second intervals, stirring at each interval, until melted. Stir until smooth. Cool slightly and pour into a resealable plastic bag. Cut a small corner off one side of the bag. Drizzle melted chocolate over cooled bars. Let chocolate cool. Cut into bars or break into irregular pieces.

Yield: 12 bars

Zowee Zucchini Squares

¼ cup (28 g) flax meal

1 cup (200 g) sugar, honey (340 g),
   or pure maple syrup (235 ml)

¼ cup (60 ml) vegetable oil

2 cups (250 g) Bob's Red Mill brown
   rice flour or certified gluten-free
   oat flour

½ cup (50 g) rice bran

1 teaspoon (2.3 g) ground cinnamon

¼ teaspoon (0.6 g) ground
   nutmeg (optional)

½ teaspoon (2.3 g) baking soda

¼ teaspoon (1.2 g) baking powder

¼ teaspoon (1.5 g) salt

1 cup (110 g) finely shredded small,
   tender zucchini

½ cup (75 g) Enjoy Life's Not Nuts!
   Beach Bash trail mix

½ cup (80 g) crushed pineapple,
   drained

DIRECTIONS

- Preheat oven to 350°F (180°C, or gas mark 4).
- Combine flax and next 9 ingredients (through salt) and mix on low. Batter will
  be lumpy. Stir in the shredded zucchini, trail mix, and crushed pineapple.
- Pour batter into a greased 9 x 13-inch (23 x 33-cm) baking pan.
- Bake for about 35 minutes. Let cool and cut into bars.

Yield: About 2 dozen

Crazy Good Caramel Chocolate Bars

FOR BARS

2 tablespoons (30 ml) vegetable oil

1 cup (225 g) packed brown sugar

2 teaspoons (10 ml) vanilla extract

1/4 cup (60 ml) water

Dash of salt

1 3/4 cups (220 g) Bob's Red Mill white rice flour

1/4 cup (60 g) Bob's Red Mill tapioca flour

1 teaspoon (4.6 g) baking powder

FOR TOPPING

1/4 cup (50 g) Spectrum Organic Shortening

1/2 cup (115 g) packed dark brown sugar

1 tablespoon (15 ml) rice milk or safe milk alternative

2 teaspoons (10 ml) real maple syrup

1 cup (120 g) powdered sugar (contains cornstarch; can use corn-free recipe on page 43)

2 cups (350 g) Enjoy Life semi-sweet chocolate chips

DIRECTIONS

- Preheat oven to 350°F (180°C, or gas mark 4).
- To make the bars: In a medium saucepan, combine oil, brown sugar, vanilla, water, and salt. Cook over low heat until smooth, about 30 seconds. Combine remaining bar ingredients in a bowl. Add the brown sugar mixture and mix until smooth.
- Spread into a greased 9 x 13-inch (23 x 33-cm) baking pan.
- Bake 35 minutes, until sides are golden and center is soft to the touch. Let cool.
- To make the topping: In a saucepan over medium-low heat, stir together the shortening, brown sugar, and rice milk. When mixture has dissolved (about 45 seconds), remove from heat. Stir in maple syrup. Add the powdered sugar, stirring constantly. Beat until smooth and of spreading consistency. If caramel becomes too stiff, stir in additional rice milk, 1 teaspoon (5 ml) at a time.
- Spread caramel mixture over the crust. Generously sprinkle the chocolate chips over the caramel. Cool and cut into bars.

Yield: About 2 dozen

Ludicrously Lemon Bars

FOR CRUST

$\frac{1}{2}$ cup (120 ml) lemon juice
    concentrate

1 teaspoon (1.7 g) lemon zest

$\frac{1}{2}$ cup (100 g) Spectrum
    Organic Shortening

1 cup (125 g) Bob's Red Mill white
    rice flour

$\frac{1}{2}$ cup (65 g) cornstarch
    (contains corn; can use tapioca or
    arrowroot starch instead)

$\frac{1}{2}$ cup (60 g) powdered sugar
    (contains cornstarch; can use corn-
    free recipe on page 43)

$\frac{1}{8}$ teaspoon (0.6 g) baking powder

$\frac{1}{8}$ teaspoon (0.8 g) salt

FOR LEMON FILLING

$\frac{1}{2}$ cup (65 g) cornstarch (contains
    corn; can use tapioca or arrowroot
    starch instead)

1 $\frac{1}{4}$ cups (250 g) superfine sugar

1 cup (235 ml) water

1 $\frac{1}{2}$ cups (355 ml) lemon juice

1 teaspoon (1.7 g) lemon zest

FOR TOPPING

Powdered sugar (contains
    cornstarch; can use corn-free
    recipe on page 43)

DIRECTIONS

- Preheat oven to 350°F (180°C, or gas mark 4).
- To make the crust: Combine all crust ingredients in a food processor and process until dough forms into a ball.
- Press crust into a greased 9 x 13-inch (23 x 33-cm) baking pan. Bake for 25 minutes. Let cool.
- To make the lemon filling: Combine starch, sugar, water, lemon juice, and lemon zest in a saucepan. Over medium heat, bring to a gentle boil while stirring constantly. Lower the heat and cook for about one minute, continuing to stir. Pour lemon mixture over crust. Let cool and then place in the refrigerator to cool completely.
- Sift powdered sugar heavily over lemon mixture. Cut into bars.

Yield: About 2 dozen

RECIPE NOTE

For Ludicrously Lemon Berry Bars, spread 1 cup (145 g) of berries (blueberries, raspberries, or cranberries) over cooked crust before pouring the lemon filling over it.

Recipe does not work well with blended flour mix.

Just Great Ginger-cake Bars

FOR BARS

1/2 cup (100 g) Spectrum
 Organic Shortening

2 tablespoons (30 g) brown sugar

1 cup (235 ml) unsulfured molasses

1 cup (235 ml) boiling water

2 cups (250 g) Bob's Red Mill white
 or brown rice flour

1/4 cup (30 g) Bob's Red Mill
 tapioca flour

1 teaspoon (4.6 g) baking soda

1/2 teaspoon (3 g) salt

1 teaspoon (1.8 g) ground ginger

1 teaspoon (2.3 g) ground cinnamon

FOR TOPPING

1 cup (250 g) sweetened chunky
 cinnamon applesauce

OR

1/3 cup (67 g) Spectrum
 Organic Shortening

2 1/2 cups (300 g) powdered sugar
 (contains cornstarch; can use
 corn-free recipe on page 43)

2 tablespoons (30 ml) water

DIRECTIONS

- Preheat oven to 325°F (170°C, or gas mark 3).
- To make the bars: With a mixer, on low speed, mix together shortening, brown sugar, molasses, and water. Add remaining bar ingredients and mix until smooth. Pour into a greased 9 x 13-inch (23 x 33-cm) baking pan.
- Bake for about 50 minutes, or until firm in the center. Let cool.
- To make the topping: Spread applesauce over the warm cake and cut into bars. Or in a food processor, combine shortening, powdered sugar, and water and pulse until smooth. Frost cake, and then cut into bars.

Yield: About 2 dozen

Ginger-iffic Bars

¼ cup (85 g) unsulfured molasses

½ cup (125 g) unsweetened applesauce

1 ½ cups (345 g) packed brown sugar

¼ cup (28 g) flax meal

1 teaspoon (5 ml) vanilla

2 cups (250 g) Bob's Red Mill brown rice flour

2 teaspoons (9.2 g) baking powder

2 teaspoons (3.6 g) ground ginger

1 teaspoon (2.3 g) ground cinnamon

¼ cup (35 g) crystallized ginger, sliced into small pieces

Powdered sugar (contains cornstarch; can use corn-free recipe on page 43

DIRECTIONS

- Preheat oven to 350°F (180°C, or gas mark 4).
- In a saucepan stir together molasses, applesauce, brown sugar, flax, and vanilla. Cook over low heat until well combined, about 1 minute. Remove from heat. Blend in flour and next 3 ingredients (through cinnamon) until smooth. Stir in crystallized ginger.
- Pour into a greased 9 x 13-inch (23 x 33-cm) baking pan.
- Bake for 30 to 35 minutes. Center will be soft and will sink slightly. Let cool completely. Sift powdered sugar over top. Cut into bars.

Yield: About 2 dozen

Fruit Jamboree Bars

MMM! One of my favorite treats!

FOR COOKIE BASE

½ cup (115 g) packed brown sugar

½ cup (60 g) Bob's Red Mill
   tapioca flour

1 cup (125 g) Bob's Red Mill white or
   brown rice flour

½ teaspoon (1.2 g) ground cinnamon

½ teaspoon (2.3 g) baking powder

Dash of salt

¼ cup (60 ml) vegetable oil

¼ cup (60 ml) water

FOR STREUSEL TOPPING

¼ cup (60 ml) vegetable oil

1 cup (225 g) packed brown sugar

1 tablespoon (30 ml) water

½ cup (60 g) Bob's Red Mill white
   or brown rice flour

1 cup (80 g) certified gluten-free
   rolled oats, rolled rice, quinoa, or
   buckwheat flakes

¼ cup (30 g) Bob's Red Mill
   tapioca flour

1 teaspoon (2.3 g) ground cinnamon

FOR FILLING

1 jar (10.25 ounce, or 287 g) of your
   choice of safe jam or preserves,
   such as strawberry, apricot, blackberry, blueberry, etc.

DIRECTIONS

- Preheat oven to 350°F (180°C, or gas mark 4).
- To make the cookie base: Combine all cookie base ingredients in a food processor and process until dough is smooth. Press dough into a greased 9 x 13-inch (23 x 33-cm) pan. Wet your hands if dough is too sticky.
- Bake for 10 minutes. Set aside to cool. Do not turn off oven.
- To make the streusel topping: In a food processor (no need to clean from previous use from cookie base), add topping ingredients and pulse mixture until it resembles pieces the size of peas. Set aside.
- Spread filling over cooled crust.
- Sprinkle streusel topping all over the preserves. Bake for 30 to 35 minutes, or until golden on top. Cool for one hour or until room temperature. Cover and place in the refrigerator. When chilled, cut into bars.

Yield: About 2 dozen

Rain Forest Fruit Bars

This is a nice treat for those kids who like fresh fruit—or for those parents who want their kids to eat more fresh fruit!

FOR CRUST

3 cups (220 g) Enjoy Life Perky's "Nutty" Rice Cereal

½ cup (120 ml) vegetable oil

¼ cup (50 g) superfine sugar

¼ cup (85 g) honey or (60 ml) pure maple syrup

½ teaspoon (3 g) salt

¼ cup (30 g) Bob's Red Mill tapioca flour

FOR ORANGE FILLING

⅓ cup (67 g) Spectrum Organic Shortening

2 ½ cups (300 g) powdered sugar (contains cornstarch; can use corn-free recipe on page 43)

¼ cup (60 ml) orange juice

1 tablespoon (5 g) orange zest

FOR TOPPING

1 peach, sliced into small pieces

½ cup (87 g) fresh diced mango

½ cup (85 g) sliced strawberries

1 kiwi, peeled and sliced

½ cup (73 g) fresh blueberries

1 tablespoon (15 ml) lemon juice

1 tablespoon (13 g) superfine sugar

1 cup (75 g) Enjoy Life Perky's "Nutty" Rice cereal

DIRECTIONS

- Preheat oven to 325°F (170°C, or gas mark 3).
- To make the crust: Place cereal in food processor and process until mixture reaches the consistency of cornmeal. Add remaining crust ingredients and pulse until cereal crumbs are well coated. Press mixture into a 9-inch (23-cm) square baking pan.
- Bake for 10 to 15 minutes. Let cool.
- To make the orange filling: Combine all filling ingredients in a food processor and pulse until smooth. Spread over cooled crust.
- To make the topping: Combine the fresh fruit in a large bowl. Pour the lemon juice and sugar over fruit and gently stir. Spoon fruit mixture over orange filling. Sprinkle 1 cup cereal over bars. Cover and place in the refrigerator to chill. Cut into bars.

Yield: About 2 dozen

Lovely Lemon Raspberry Bites

These make great muffins or mini muffins.

1 1/2 cups (355 ml) lemonade

1 cup (200 g) sugar

1/4 cup (60 ml) vegetable oil

1 teaspoon (5 ml) vanilla

3 cups (375 g) Bob's Red Mill
white rice flour

1 tablespoon (13.8 g) baking powder

1/2 teaspoon (3 g) salt

1 1/2 cups (165 g) fresh or frozen
raspberries, thawed

DIRECTIONS

• Preheat oven to 350°F (180°C, or gas mark 4).

• In a large bowl, mix together lemonade and next 6 ingredients (through salt) until smooth. Stir in raspberries.

• Pour into greased or paper-lined mini muffin pans.

• Bake for about 15-20 minutes, or until the centers feel firm to the touch. Let cool and remove from tin. Sprinkle with powdered sugar if desired.

Yield: About 2 dozen

Yikes Stripes Brownies

One of my testers' favorite brownies.

FOR BROWNIES

¹/₂ cup (125 g) unsweetened
    applesauce

2 tablespoons (30 ml) vegetable oil

1 cup (200 g) superfine sugar

¹/₄ teaspoon (1.5 g) salt

1 cup (175 g) Enjoy Life semi-sweet
    chocolate chips

1 teaspoon (5 ml) vanilla extract

¹/₃ cup (29 g) unsweetened cocoa

¹/₄ cup (60 ml) water

1 ¹/₂ cups (185 g) Bob's Red Mill white
    or brown rice flour

¹/₃ cup (42 g) Bob's Red Mill
    tapioca flour

¹/₂ teaspoon (2.3 g) baking soda

FOR FROSTING STRIPES

1 cup (120 g) powdered sugar
    (contains cornstarch; can use
    corn-free recipe on page 43)

2 tablespoons (25 g) Spectrum
    Organic Shortening

1 tablespoon (15 ml) vanilla extract

1 teaspoon (5 ml) water

DIRECTIONS

- Preheat oven to 350°F (180°C, or gas mark 4).
- To make the brownies: In a large saucepan combine applesauce, oil, sugar, salt, chocolate chips, vanilla, cocoa, and water. Cook over low heat, stirring constantly until chocolate chips are melted. Remove from heat.
- Stir in remaining brownie ingredients. Pour into a greased 9 x 13-inch (23 x 33-cm) baking pan.
- Bake for about 25 minutes, or until slightly soft in the center and more firm around the edges. Let cool completely.
- To make the frosting stripes: Combine all frosting ingredients in a bowl and mix together with a whisk. Place frosting in a resealable plastic bag and cut off a small corner. Make frosting stripes across the top of the brownie. Cut into bars.

Yield: About 2 dozen

Marvelous Maple Bars

FOR BARS

¼ cup (50 g) Spectrum
   Organic Shortening

1 cup (235 ml) pure maple syrup

1 cup (225 g) packed brown sugar

1 cup (125 g) Bob's Red Mill
   sorghum flour

1 ½ cups (185 g) Bob's Red Mill white
   or brown rice flour

½ cup (60 g) Bob's Red Mill
   tapioca flour

2 teaspoons (9.2 g) baking soda

FOR FROSTING

1 ½ cups (180 g) powdered sugar
   (contains cornstarch; can use
   corn-free recipe on page 43)

¼ cup (60 ml) pure maple syrup

DIRECTIONS

- Preheat oven to 350°F (180°C, or gas mark 4).
- To make the bars: Cream together shortening, syrup, and brown sugar. Add the remaining bar ingredients and blend until smooth. Pour into a greased 9 x 13-inch (23 x 33-cm) baking pan.
- Bake for 30 minutes, or until golden around the edges. Let cool.
- To make the frosting: Mix powdered sugar and maple syrup in a bowl. Add a little water if needed to achieve desired consistency. Frost bars and cut into squares.

Yield: About 2 dozen

Chocolate-Lovers' Shortbread Sticks

FOR SHORTBREAD

$\frac{1}{2}$ cup (100 g) Spectrum
  Organic Shortening

1 cup (125 g) Bob's Red Mill white
  rice flour

$\frac{1}{2}$ cup (65 g) cornstarch (contains
  corn; can use tapioca or arrowroot
  starch instead)

$\frac{1}{2}$ cup (60 g) powdered sugar
  (contains cornstarch; can use
  corn-free recipe on page 43)

$\frac{1}{8}$ teaspoon (0.6 g) baking powder

$\frac{1}{8}$ teaspoon (0.8 g) salt

1 teaspoon (5 ml) vanilla

$\frac{1}{4}$ cup (65 g) melted chocolate

FOR CHOCOLATE TOPPING

2 (1.4-ounce, or 40-g) Enjoy Life
  boom CHOCO boom dark
  chocolate bars

1 teaspoon (0.3 g) Spectrum
  Organic Shortening

DIRECTIONS

- Preheat oven to 350°F (180°C, or gas mark 4).
- To make the shortbread: In a food processor, combine all shortbread ingredients and process for 1 minute. Use your hands to form dough into a rectangle. Cut dough into 1-inch (2.5-cm) sticks. Place each stick on a greased baking sheet.
- Bake for about 15 minutes, or until edges are golden; the centers should not be browned. Let sit for half an hour on baking sheet to cool.
- To make the chocolate topping: In a microwave-safe bowl, break the chocolate bars into tiny pieces. Microwave at 30-second intervals, stirring at every interval until melted and smooth. Stir in shortening. Cool slightly. Dip each shortbread stick halfway into the chocolate topping. Set on a foil-lined baking sheet and cool until chocolate hardens.

Yield: 12 sticks

RECIPE NOTE

Recipe does not work well with blended flour mix.

Cranny Banana Bars

These bars have a mixture of so many wonderful flavors.
I make them often during the holiday season.

FOR BARS

1 cup (225 g) packed brown sugar

2 bananas, sliced

1/3 cup (80 ml) vegetable oil

1/4 cup (60 g) unsweetened
   applesauce

6 tablespoons (90 ml) orange juice

1 cup (125 g) Bob's Red Mill white
   or brown rice flour

1/2 cup (60 g) Bob's Red Mill
   tapioca flour

1 teaspoon (4.6 g) baking powder

Dash of salt

1/3 cup (50 g) dried cranberries

1 teaspoon (1.7 g) lemon or orange
   zest (optional)

FOR GLAZE

1/2 cup (60 g) powdered sugar
   (contains cornstarch; can use
   corn-free recipe on page 43)

1 tablespoon (15 ml) orange juice

1 teaspoon (1.7 g) lemon or orange
   zest (optional)

DIRECTIONS

- Preheat oven to 350°F (180°C, or gas mark 4).
- To make the bars: With a mixer, cream together brown sugar, bananas, oil, apple-sauce, and juice. Mixture will be a little lumpy. Add in the flours, baking powder, and salt and mix until smooth. Stir in the cranberries and zest, if using. Pour into a 9 x 13-inch (23 x 33-cm) baking pan.
- Bake for about 40 minutes, or until firm in the center. Let cool.
- To make the glaze: Whisk together powdered sugar, juice, and zest, if using. With a spoon, drizzle the glaze over the cooled cake. Cut into bars.

Yield: About 2 dozen

Sunny Cinnamon Bars

These are easy to make, flavorful, and reminiscent of coffee cake. For an extra crunch, stir ½ cup (41.2 g) of crushed granola into batter.

FOR BARS

1 cup (245 g) unsweetened applesauce

1 cup (225 g) packed brown sugar

½ cup (120 ml) vegetable oil

1 tablespoon (7 g) ground cinnamon

¼ cup (60 ml) water

1 ½ cups (185 g) Bob's Red Mill white or brown rice flour

½ cup (60 g) Bob's Red Mill tapioca flour

Dash of salt

2 teaspoons (9.2 g) baking powder

½ cup (68 g) unsalted sunflower seed kernels

1 cup (165 g) sulfite-free packed golden raisins

FOR TOPPING

1 teaspoon (2.3 g) ground cinnamon plus ¼ cup (50 g) sugar.

OR

1 cup (82 g) Enjoy Life Cranapple Crunch Granola

DIRECTIONS

- Preheat oven to 350°F (180°C, or gas mark 4).
- To make the bars: Mix together applesauce, brown sugar, oil, and cinnamon. Add water and next 4 ingredients (through baking powder) and blend until smooth. Stir in the sunflower seeds and raisins. Pour into a 8-inch (20-cm) square baking pan.
- To make the topping: Combine cinnamon and sugar in a bowl and sprinkle over top of dough. Or, if using granola, place granola in a sealed plastic bag. Roll a rolling pin over bag to break granola into tiny pieces. Sprinkle over top of dough.
- Bake for about 40 minutes, or until firm in the center. Let cool and cut into squares.

Yield: About 2 dozen

Call of the Wild Rice Spice Bars

FOR BARS

1 ³/₄ cups (430 g) unsweetened
   applesauce

1 cup (165 g) precooked wild or
   brown rice

¹/₂ cup (100 g) Spectrum
   Organic Shortening

³/₄ cup (170 g) packed brown sugar

1 cup (125 g) Bob's Red Mill brown
   rice or sorghum flour

¹/₂ cup (60 g) Bob's Red Mill
   tapioca flour

1 teaspoon (4.6 g) baking soda

1 teaspoon (2.3 g) ground cinnamon

¹/₂ teaspoon (3 g) salt

1 cup (165 g) packed sulfite-free
   raisins

FOR FROSTING

2 cups (240 g) powdered sugar
   (contains cornstarch; can use
   corn-free recipe on page 43)

2 tablespoons (25 g) Spectrum
   Organic Shortening

2 tablespoons (30 ml) rice milk or
   safe milk alternative

¹/₂ teaspoon (2.5 ml) vanilla

¹/₂ teaspoon (1.2 g) ground cinnamon

OR

Honey

DIRECTIONS

- Preheat oven to 350°F (180°C, or gas mark 4).
- To make the bars: In a small saucepan, bring the unsweetened applesauce and rice to a slow boil. Cover and let stand for 20 minutes. The rice should be very soft.
- With a mixer, cream together the shortening and brown sugar. Add in the rice flour and the next 4 ingredients (through salt) and mix slowly. Stir in raisins. Pour in the applesauce mixture and mix until you have a smooth batter. Pour batter into a greased 9 x 13-inch (23 x 33-cm) baking pan.
- Bake for 45 minutes, or until firm in the center. Cool.
- To make the frosting: Place frosting ingredients in a food processor and blend until smooth. Frost cooled bars or, alternatively, drizzle with honey.

Yield: About 2 dozen

Apple Pie Goodness Bars

A crunchy crust, cinnamon and apple filling, and a sweet topping—
who needs pie when you can whip up these bars for on the go!

FOR CRUST AND TOPPING

3 cups (220 g) Enjoy Life Perky's
   "Nutty" Rice Cereal

½ cup (120 ml) vegetable oil

¼ cup (50 g) superfine sugar

¼ cup (85 g) honey or (60 ml) pure
   maple syrup

½ teaspoon (3 g) salt

¼ cup (30 g) Bob's Red Mill
   tapioca flour

FOR APPLE FILLING

1 cup (235 ml) apple juice

1 teaspoon (2.3 g) ground cinnamon

¼ cup (60 g) packed brown sugar

3 tablespoons (24 g) cornstarch
   (contains corn; can use tapioca or
   arrowroot starch instead)

3 apples, cut into almond-
   size pieces

1 teaspoon (5 ml) vegetable oil

DIRECTIONS

• Preheat oven to 325°F (170°C, or gas mark 3).

• To make the crust: Place cereal in food processor and process until mixture
  resembles cornmeal. Add remaining crust ingredients and pulse until cereal crumbs
  are well coated. Press mixture into a greased 9-inch (23-cm) square baking pan,
  reserving ½ cup for topping.

• Bake for 10 to 15 minutes. Let cool.

• To make the apple filling: Mix together apple juice, cinnamon, brown sugar, and
  starch in a medium saucepan. Add in apples and oil. Cook over low heat, stirring
  occasionally, until thick and bubbly.

• Pour over crust. Sprinkle reserved topping over apple mixture.

• Return to oven for 15 minutes. Cool completely and cut into bars.

Yield: About 2 dozen

Pump Me Up Pumpkin Pie Bars

FOR CRUST

1 cup (125 g) Bob's Red Mill white or brown rice flour

½ cup (60 g) Bob's Red Mill tapioca flour

½ cup (115 g) packed brown sugar

½ teaspoon (2.6 g) baking powder

½ teaspoon (1.2 g) ground cinnamon

Dash of salt

¼ cup (60 ml) vegetable oil

¼ cup (60 ml) warm water

FOR FILLING

¾ cup (170 g) packed brown sugar

2 teaspoons (4 g) pumpkin pie spice (or make your own; see page 42)

¼ teaspoon (1.5 g) salt

3 tablespoons (24 g) cornstarch (contains corn; can use tapioca or arrowroot starch instead)

1 can (15-ounce, or 427 g) pumpkin

1 cup (235 ml) rice milk or safe milk alternative

FOR TOPPING

1 ½ cups (123 g) Enjoy Life Cranapple Crunch Granola

OR

½ cup (60 g) powdered sugar (contains cornstarch; can use corn-free recipe on page 43)

DIRECTIONS

- Preheat oven to 350°F (180°C, or gas mark 4).
- To make the crust: In a food processor, combine all crust ingredients. Process for about 1 minute, or until dough rolls into a ball. Press dough into a greased 9 x 13-inch (23 x 33-cm) baking pan, pressing dough halfway up the sides of the pan.
- To make the filling: Combine all filling ingredients in a large bowl; pour over dough.
- To make the topping: In a food processor, pulse granola until it is the size of rolled oats. Sprinkle evenly over the uncooked pie.
- Bake for about 1 hour, or until sides are golden and center is soft to the touch. If granola is browning too quickly, cover with aluminum foil. Cool completely. If not using granola topping, dust with powdered sugar. Cut into bars.

Yield: About 2 dozen

Pineapple Perfect Upside-Down Bars

FOR TOPPING

2 tablespoons (30 ml) vegetable oil

2 teaspoons (10 ml) water

1/2 cup (115 g) packed brown sugar

1 can (15–ounce, or 427 g) mini or
regular pineapple rings, well drained,
or 1 sliced fresh peach or apple

FOR BARS

1/3 cup (80 ml) vegetable oil

2/3 cup (160 ml) rice milk, safe milk
alternative, or water

1 teaspoon (5 ml) vanilla extract

1/2 teaspoon (3 g) salt

1 cup (125 g) Bob's Red Mill white
or brown rice flour

1/2 cup (60 g) Bob's Red Mill
tapioca flour

1 cup (225 g) packed brown sugar

2 teaspoons (9.2 g) baking powder

DIRECTIONS

- Preheat oven to 350°F (180°C, or gas mark 4).
- To make the topping: In a small saucepan, heat the oil, water, and brown sugar until smooth and caramel-like (about 1 minute).
- Line a 9 x 13-inch (23 x 33-cm) baking pan with aluminum foil or nonstick parchment paper. Pour caramel mixture into bottom of the lined pan. Arrange the drained pineapple rings or fruit over the caramel sauce.
- To make the bars: In a large bowl, mix together the bar ingredients until you have a smooth dough. Pour over arranged pineapple rings.
- Bake for 45 minutes, or until lightly golden and semi-firm in the center. Let cool.
- Place a flat plate or cutting board directly over the baking pan. Flip over and remove baking pan. Gently remove aluminum foil on top. Note that the caramel sauce is very hot. Be careful when peeling off the foil. Cut into squares. Fill the holes of the pineapple rings with cherries, raisins, or sunflower seed kernels for extra décor.

Yield: 12 bars

Heavenly Honey-Lemon Bars

These traditional Greek cake bars are usually decorated with sesame seeds,
but here we replace them with golden flaxseeds.

FOR BARS

¼ cup (85 g) flower-flavored or
   regular honey

Juice and grated rind of 1 lemon

⅔ cup (160 ml) rice milk or safe
   milk alternative

3 tablespoons (45 ml) vegetable oil

Dash of salt

2 ¼ cups (280 g) Bob's Red Mill white
   rice flour

⅔ cup (83 g) Bob's Red Mill
   tapioca flour

1 teaspoon (4.6 g) baking powder

¼ teaspoon (0.6 g) grated nutmeg

2 teaspoons (9 g) golden flaxseeds
   or sunflower seed kernels (or a
   combination of both)

FOR TOPPING

1 tablespoon (21 g) honey

1 tablespoon (15 ml) lemon juice

DIRECTIONS

- Preheat oven to 375°F (190°C, or gas mark 5).
- To make the bars: In a small bowl, combine honey, lemon juice, and milk and stir. Set aside.
- In a large bowl, place oil and next 5 ingredients (through nutmeg). With mixer on low slowly add the honey-milk mixture. Blend until smooth. Pour batter into a greased 9 x 13-inch (23 x 33-cm) baking pan. Sprinkle flaxseeds over cake.
- Bake for 30 minutes, or until golden brown.
- To make the topping: In a small bowl, whisk together the honey and the lemon juice. Drizzle over warm cake. Cut cake into thin "finger" bars.

Yield: About 2 dozen

Peppermint Pizzazz Brownies

FOR BROWNIES

$1/2$ cup (125 g) unsweetened
  applesauce

2 tablespoons (30 ml) vegetable oil

1 cup (200 g) superfine sugar

$1/4$ teaspoon (1.5 g) salt

1 cup (175 g) Enjoy Life semi-sweet
  chocolate chips

1 teaspoon (5 ml) vanilla extract

$1/3$ cup (28.7 g) unsweetened cocoa

$1/4$ cup (60 ml) water

$1/4$ teaspoon (1.3 ml) peppermint
  extract

$1 1/2$ cups (185 g) Bob's Red Mill white
  or brown rice flour

$1/3$ cup (42 g) Bob's Red Mill
  tapioca flour

$1/2$ teaspoon (2.3 g) baking soda

FOR FROSTING

1 cup (120 g) powdered sugar
  (contains cornstarch; can use
  corn-free recipe on page 43)

2 tablespoons (25 g) Spectrum
  Organic Shortening

$1/2$ teaspoon (2.5 ml) peppermint
  extract

1 teaspoon (5 ml) water

DIRECTIONS

- Preheat oven to 350°F (180°C, or gas mark 4).
- To make the brownies: In a large saucepan, combine applesauce, oil, sugar, salt, chocolate chips, vanilla, cocoa, water, and peppermint. Over low heat, stir constantly until chocolate chips are melted. Remove from heat.
- Stir in remaining ingredients. Pour batter into a greased 9 x 13-inch (23 x 33-cm) baking pan.
- Bake for about 25 minutes, or until slightly soft in the center and firmer around the edges. Let cool completely.
- To make the frosting: Combine all frosting ingredients in a bowl and mix with a whisk. Frost the top of the cooled brownie. Cut into bars.

Yield: About 2 dozen

Especially Espresso Brownies

FOR BROWNIES

$\frac{1}{3}$ cup (80 ml) brewed strong coffee
  or espresso

1 cup (200 g) superfine sugar

$\frac{1}{4}$ cup (60 ml) vegetable oil

$\frac{1}{4}$ cup (60 ml) water

$\frac{1}{4}$ cup (60 g) applesauce

1 cup (175 g) Enjoy Life semi-sweet
  chocolate chips

$\frac{3}{4}$ cup (94 g) Bob's Red Mill white
  rice flour

$\frac{1}{4}$ cup (31 g) Bob's Red Mill
  tapioca flour

$\frac{1}{2}$ teaspoon (2.3 g) baking powder

Dash of salt

FOR FROSTING

$\frac{1}{2}$ cup (120 ml) rice milk or safe
  milk alternative

$\frac{1}{4}$ cup (60 ml) brewed strong coffee
  or espresso

1 cup (175 g) Enjoy Life semi-sweet
  chocolate chips

1 $\frac{1}{2}$ cups (180 g) powdered sugar
  (contains cornstarch; can use
  corn-free recipe on page 43)

DIRECTIONS

- Preheat oven to 350°F (180°C, or gas mark 4).
- To make the brownies: In a saucepan, combine coffee, sugar, oil, water, applesauce, and chocolate chips. Over low heat, stir frequently until chocolate chips are melted. Add remaining bar ingredients and stir until smooth. Pour batter into a greased 9-inch (23-cm) square baking pan.
- Bake for about 25 to 30 minutes, or until semi-firm in the center. Let cool.
- To make the frosting: Heat milk, coffee, and chocolate chips in a saucepan over low heat, stirring until smooth. Add powdered sugar and stir until smooth. Spread over brownie. Cut into squares or bars.

Yield: 12 bars

Berry Yummy Peach Bars

*Even though these are bar cookies, it is best to eat them warm
like a cobbler with a bowl and spoon!*

FOR FRUIT FILLING

1 can (15-ounce, or 427 g) can of
sliced peaches (in juice)

¼ cup (60 g) raw sugar or packed
brown sugar

2 tablespoons (16 g) cornstarch
(contains corn; can use tapioca or
arrowroot starch instead)

1 cup (145 g) blueberries

1 cup (145 g) blackberries

FOR CRUST AND TOPPING

1 package (6 ounce, or 170 g)
Enjoy Life Snickerdoodle cookies

3 tablespoons (37 g) Spectrum
Organic Shortening

1 teaspoon (5 ml) vanilla extract

⅓ cup (75 g) packed brown sugar

DIRECTIONS

- Preheat oven to 350°F (180°C, or gas mark 4).

- To make the fruit filling: In a large bowl, mix together juice from peaches, sugar,
and starch. Stir in fruit. Place in a saucepan and cook over low heat until mixture
thickens. Set aside.

- To make the crust and topping: Combine crust ingredients in a food processor.
Pulse until the mixture resembles flax meal. Press half of the crust mixture into a
greased 8-inch (20-cm) square baking pan. Reserve the other half of the crust mixture for the topping. Pour the fruit mixture over the crust. Take the reserved crust
mixture and sprinkle over the fruit mixture.

- Bake for about 20 minutes, or until the topping is golden and the fruit mixture is
dark purple and thick. Let cool for 30 minutes before cutting into bars.

Yield: About 2 dozen

Chapter 7

No-Bake Cookies, Tartlets, and other Bite-Size Goodies

This is my favorite section. These delicious treats are creative and fun to present to your kids, family and friends. You will find a variety of treats to satisfy any tastebuds!

Have a tea party with your wee ones, or plan a tea party with other
mommies while the wee ones play. This is the perfect sweet
to enjoy with tea and good company.

Wholesome 'n Hearty Tartlet Crust

*This super-sturdy crust tastes like whole wheat and is great
for pumpkin, apple, and savory crust tartlets.*

INGREDIENTS

1 ½ cups (185 g) Bob's Red Mill
   white or brown rice flour or
   sorghum flour*

¼ cup (60 ml) vegetable oil

¼ teaspoon (1.5 g) salt

1 tablespoon (15 ml) pure maple syrup

¼ cup (28 g) flax meal

⅓ cup (42 g) Bob's Red Mill
   tapioca flour

¼ cup (60 ml) water, plus more
   if needed

DIRECTIONS

- Preheat oven to 350°F (180°C, or gas mark 4).
- Place all ingredients in a food processor. Pulse until you have a firm dough that forms a ball. If mixture is too dry, add water 1 teaspoon (5 ml) at a time.
- Pinch off 2 to 3 teaspoons (10 g to 16 g) of dough and roll it to form a ball. Repeat with remaining dough. Wet your hands if needed to keep dough from sticking. Press each dough ball into one cup of a greased mini muffin pan or a mini tartlet pan.
- Bake for about 25 minutes, or until the mini crust pulls easily out of the muffin tin. They should not be golden or discolored. Remove all crusts from the muffin tin and let cool on a flat surface. Cool completely or refrigerate until ready to fill.

Yield: 42 tartlets

*If using sorghum flour, increase water to ½ cup (120 ml)

Sweet 'n Tender Tartlet Crust

*These crusts have great flavor and hold a perfect shape for
your sweet pies and ice cream desserts.*

³/₄ cup (94 g) Bob's Red Mill white
   rice flour

¹/₃ cup (42 g) Bob's Red Mill
   tapioca flour

2 tablespoons (26 g) superfine sugar

¹/₄ teaspoon (1.3 ml) baking powder

¹/₄ teaspoon (1.3 g) distilled
   white vinegar

¹/₄ teaspoon (1.5 g) salt

¹/₄ cup (60 ml) vegetable oil

³/₈ to ¹/₂ cup (90 to 120 ml)
   warm water

DIRECTIONS

- Preheat oven to 350°F (180°C, or gas mark 4).
- In a food processor, combine all ingredients except water. Add in ³/₈ cup (90 ml) of warm water. Process for about 1 minute, or until dough rolls into a ball. If dough is too dry and is not forming into a ball, add an additional ¹/₈ cup (30 ml) of water.
- Pinch off about 2 teaspoons (10 g) of dough and roll into a ball. Press into a greased mini muffin pan.
- Bake for about 25 minutes, or until the crusts pull easily out of the muffin tin. They should not be golden or discolored. Remove all crusts from the muffin tin and let cool on a flat surface. Cool completely or refrigerate until ready to fill.

Yield: 42 tartlets

Here are a few choices for your tartlets. Be creative and invent your own favorite combinations. Refrigerate leftover filling in a sealed plastic container for a yummy, creamy treat for later.

Pumped Up Pumpkin

Used unbaked tartlet shells for these tasty treats.

¾ cup (170 g) packed brown sugar

1 tablespoon (6 g) pumpkin pie spice (or make your own; see page 42)

¼ teaspoon (1.5 g) salt

¼ cup (32 g) cornstarch (contains corn; can use tapioca or arrowroot starch instead)

1 can (15 ounce, or 427-g) can pumpkin or 1 ¾ cups (430 g) cooked fresh pumpkin

1 cup (235 ml) rice milk or safe milk alternative

DIRECTIONS

• Preheat oven to 350°F (180°C, or gas mark 4).

• In a large bowl mix together all ingredients until smooth. Spoon into unbaked tartlet shells (see recipe on page 146). Bake for 40 minutes.

Yield: 42 tartlets

Dreamy "Creamy" Chocolate

2 (1.4-ounce, or 40 g) Enjoy Life
    boom CHOCO boom dark chocolate
    or dairy-free rice milk bars
1 ½ cups (355 ml) rice milk or safe
    milk alternative, divided

¼ cup (50 g) superfine sugar
2 tablespoons (16 g) cornstarch
    (contains corn; can use tapioca
    or arrowroot starch instead)

DIRECTIONS

- Break the chocolate bars into pieces and combine with 1 cup (235 ml) rice milk in a small saucepan. Over medium-low heat, melt the chocolate with the milk while stirring constantly.
- In a small bowl, whisk together the remaining ½ cup (120 ml) rice milk with the sugar and starch.
- Remove saucepan from heat and whisk the starch mixture into the chocolate mixture. Return to stovetop over medium heat and bring to a low boil. Once mixture is thick and bubbly, remove from heat. Let cool for 5 minutes, stirring occasionally. Spoon mixture into prebaked tartlet shells (see recipe on page 147).

Yield: 42 tartlets

Strawberries & "Cream"

2 ³/₄ cups (645 ml) rice milk or safe
   milk alternative
¹/₄ cup (50 g) superfine sugar
3 tablespoons (108 g) Kraft
   Minute Tapioca

1 teaspoon (5 ml) vanilla extract
1 cup (170 g) sliced strawberries
Whole strawberries, for garnish
   (optional)

DIRECTIONS

- Stir together the milk, sugar, and tapioca in a medium saucepan. Let stand 5 minutes. Cook over medium heat until mixture comes to full boil, stirring constantly. Remove from heat. Stir in vanilla. Cool 20 minutes. Stir in strawberries. Spoon into prebaked tartlet shells (see recipe on page 147). Refrigerate until thoroughly chilled.

Yield: 42 tartlets

Raspberries & "Cream"

2 ³/₄ cups (645 ml) rice milk or safe
   milk alternative
¹/₄ cup (50 g) superfine sugar
3 tablespoons (108 g) Kraft
   Minute Tapioca

1 teaspoon (5 ml) vanilla extract
1 cup (110 g) fresh raspberries,
   plus extra for garnish

DIRECTIONS

- Stir together the milk, sugar, and tapioca in a medium saucepan. Let stand 5 minutes. Cook over medium heat until mixture comes to full boil, stirring constantly. Remove from heat. Stir in vanilla. Cool 20 minutes. Stir in raspberries. Spoon into prebaked tartlet shells (see recipe on page 147). Refrigerate until thoroughly chilled.

Yield: 42 tartlets

Bananas & "Cream"

2 ³/₄ cups (645 ml) rice milk or safe
   milk alternative

¼ cup (50 g) superfine sugar

3 tablespoons (108 g) Kraft
   Minute Tapioca

1 teaspoon (5 ml) vanilla extract

1 cup (225 g) sliced firm (not brown)
   bananas, about 2

DIRECTIONS

• Stir together the milk, sugar, and tapioca in a medium saucepan. Let stand 5 minutes. Cook over medium heat until mixture comes to full boil, stirring constantly. Remove from heat. Stir in vanilla. Cool 20 minutes. Stir in bananas. Spoon into prebaked tartlet shells (see recipe on page 147). Refrigerate until thoroughly chilled.

Yield: 42 tartlets

"Buttery"-scotch "Cream"

¼ cup (32 g) cornstarch (contains
   corn; can use tapioca or arrowroot
   starch instead)

1 cup (235 ml) water

1 ²/₃ cups (390 ml) rice milk or safe
   milk alternative

1 cup (225 g) packed brown sugar

½ teaspoon (3 g) salt

2 teaspoons (10 ml) vanilla extract

DIRECTIONS

• Whisk together the starch and the water. In a saucepan over medium-low heat combine starch mixture, rice milk, brown sugar, and salt. Bring to a gentle boil and stir constantly as the mixture thickens. When thick and golden, remove from heat. Stir in vanilla. Pour into prebaked and cooled tartlet shells (see recipe on page 147). Let cool.

Yield: 42 tartlets

Paradise Pie

¹/₄ cup (144 g) Kraft Minute Tapioca

¹/₂ cup (100 g) superfine sugar

1 ¹/₂ cups (355 ml) water

1 teaspoon (1.7 g) grated orange peel

1 cup (235 ml) orange juice

1 small mango

1 kiwi

1 teaspoon (4 g) superfine sugar

1 teaspoon (5 ml) lemon juice

DIRECTIONS

- Mix tapioca, sugar, and water in medium saucepan. Let stand for 5 minutes. Bring to full boil over medium heat, stirring constantly. Remove from heat. Stir in orange peel and juice. Pour into a medium bowl. Place plastic wrap directly on the surface of the tapioca to keep a film from forming. Refrigerate for 1 hour or until cooled.
- Peel the mango and kiwi. Cut or slice into small, bite-size pieces. Place in a bowl and sprinkle with sugar and lemon juice. Stir and refrigerate.
- You may fill each prebaked and cooled tartlet shell (see recipe on page 147) with orange filling and place pieces of the fruit mixture on top as decoration, or else stir the fruit pieces into the orange filling and then fill the tartlet shells.

Yield: 42 tartlets

I Scream Delight Cups

2 pints of your favorite Rice Cream® or safe ice cream alternative

Decorations, such as Enjoy Life semi-sweet chocolate chips, fresh berries, fruit sauce, or melted chocolate

DIRECTIONS

- Fill each tartlet shell (see recipe on page 147) with ice cream and decorate with desired toppings. Freeze until ready to serve.

Yield: 42 tartlets

Berry-Lemon

½ cup (65 g) cornstarch (contains corn; can use tapioca or arrowroot starch instead)

1¼ cups (250 g) superfine sugar

1 cup (235 ml) water

1½ cups (355 ml) lemon juice

1 teaspoon (1.7 g) lemon zest

1 cup (145 g) small blueberries

DIRECTIONS

• Combine starch, sugar, water, lemon juice, and lemon zest in a saucepan. Bring to a gentle boil over medium heat, stirring constantly. Turn heat down and cook for about one minute, continuing to stir. Gently stir in blueberries. Pour hot mixture into pre-baked and cooled tartlet shells (see recipe on page 147). Let cool and then refrigerate.

Yield: 42 tartlets

Making Like Mince

1 orange

⅓ cup (80 ml) apple juice

1 teaspoon (2.7 g) cornstarch (contains corn; can use tapioca or arrowroot starch instead)

½ cup (82 g) packed sulfite-free raisins

4 medium apples, chopped into almond-size pieces

¾ cup (170 g) packed brown sugar

½ teaspoon (1.2 g) ground cinnamon

½ teaspoon (1 g) ground cloves

DIRECTIONS

• Juice the orange and grate the peel. Stir together the apple juice and starch. Combine juice, peel, starch mixture, and remaining ingredients in a saucepan. Simmer orange until the apples are soft and the mixture has cooked down. Cool slightly and spoon mixture into prebaked and cooled Hearty Tartlet shells (see recipe on page 146).

Yield: 42 tartlets

Cocoa Sunflower Power

1 cup (200 g) sugar

1 tablespoon (8 g) cornstarch (contains corn; can use tapioca or arrowroot starch instead)

3 tablespoons (16.2 g) unsweetened cocoa

1/2 teaspoon (3 g) salt

2 1/2 cups (590 ml) boiling water

2 teaspoons (10 ml) vanilla

1/3 cup (87 g) sunflower butter, chunky or smooth

DIRECTIONS

• Mix sugar, starch, cocoa, and salt together in a small saucepan. Add boiling water and vanilla, stir well, and cook over medium heat until thickened. Stir in sunflower butter. Cool and pour into prebaked and cooled tartlet shells (see recipe on page 147). Refrigerate.

Yield: 42 tartlets

Triple Treat Chocolate Tartlets

FOR CRUST

1 cup (125 g) Bob's Red Mill white rice flour

1/2 cup (65 g) cornstarch (contains corn; can use tapioca or arrowroot starch instead)

2 tablespoons (16 g) powdered sugar (contains cornstarch; can use corn-free recipe on page 43)

1/2 cup (100 g) Spectrum Organic Shortening

1/4 cup (60 ml) water

FOR CHOCOLATE FILLING

2 (1.4-ounce, or 40 g) Enjoy Life boom CHOCO boom dark chocolate bars

1 1/2 cups (355 ml) rice milk or safe milk alternative, divided

2 tablespoons (16 g) cornstarch (contains corn; can use tapioca or arrowroot starch instead)

FOR TOPPING

1 (1.4-ounce, or 40 g) Enjoy Life boom CHOCO boom dark chocolate bar

DIRECTIONS

- Preheat oven to 350°F (180°C, or gas mark 4).
- To make the crust: Combine all crust ingredients in a food processor and blend until you have a smooth dough. Pinch off a tablespoon (16 g) of dough and roll into a ball. Press each dough ball into one cup of a mini muffin pan.
- Bake for about 15 to 20 minutes. The shells should not get darker in color. When cooled they should easily lift out of the tin and hold their shape well. Remove each crust to a flat surface to cool.
- To make the filling: Break the dark chocolate bars into pieces and combine with 1 cup (235 ml) rice milk in a small saucepan. Over medium-low heat, melt the chocolate with the milk while stirring constantly.
- In a small bowl whisk together the remaining ½ cup (120 ml) rice milk with the starch. Remove saucepan from heat and whisk the starch mixture into the chocolate mixture. Return to stovetop over medium heat and bring to a low boil. Once mixture is thick and bubbly remove from heat. Let cool for 5 minutes, stirring occasionally.
- With a spoon or small ladle, pour chocolate filling into each tartlet shell.
- To make the topping: Grate the chocolate bar with a zester. Play with the different sized grates. You can make large chocolate curls or chocolate zest. Sprinkle over each tartlet.

*To make chocolate "zest," break a 1.4-ounce (40-g) chocolate bar into pieces. Place in a food processor and pulse until you get a chocolate powder with small pieces. This makes an awesome decoration for pies, frosted cookies, and cakes or bars.

Chocolicious Petit Fours

Who wouldn't want an elegant little tea treat to brighten their day or celebration? Make these easy bite-size treats when you want to make something special for your loved ones! Be creative with your decorations. I have used fresh edible flowers to place on the tops for Mother's Day, I have made these into little presents at Christmas, and I have decorated them with candies on top at Easter.

FOR PETIT FOURS

1 cup (200 g) superfine sugar

1 teaspoon (5 ml) vanilla extract

1/2 cup plus 1 tablespoon (135 ml)
   vegetable oil

1 1/4 cups (295 ml) water

2 cups (250 g) Bob's Red Mill white
   rice flour

1/2 cup (60 g) Bob's Red Mill
   tapioca flour

1 tablespoon (13.8 g) baking powder

Dash of salt

1/2 cup (43 g) unsweetened
   cocoa powder

FOR FUDGE FROSTING

1/4 cup (50 g) Spectrum
   Organic Shortening

3 tablespoons (45 ml) water

2 cups (240 g) powdered sugar
   (contains cornstarch; can use
   corn-free recipe on page 43)

2 tablespoons (11 g) unsweetened
   cocoa powder

Dash of salt

FOR WHITE FROSTING

1 cup (120 g) powdered sugar
   (contains cornstarch; can use corn-
   free recipe on page 43)

1 tablespoon (15 ml) vanilla extract

1/2 teaspoon (2.5 ml) water, if needed

DIRECTIONS

- Preheat oven to 350°F (180°C, or gas mark 4).
- To make the petit fours: In a bowl stir together sugar, vanilla, oil, and water. Add remaining ingredients and stir until smooth. Pour into a greased 9 x 13-inch (23 x 33-cm) baking pan.
- Bake for about 35 minutes, or until middle appears cracked and is firm to the touch. Let cool, then place in the refrigerator until chilled.
- Cut the chilled cake into mini squares. You may make them whatever size you choose. I try to make them small enough to fit inside a mini cupcake paper liner.
- To make the fudge frosting: Place shortening and water in a saucepan and heat until melted and smooth, about 30 seconds. Place powdered sugar, cocoa powder, and salt With a mixer,. Turn mixer on low speed and slowly pour hot shortening mixture into the mixer. When ingredients are combined, turn mixer to medium-high speed, stopping to scrape down the sides often. Mix for about 1 minute.
- While the fudge frosting is still warm, spoon or spread over the tops and sides of the cake cubes. Set on a flat surface or place in the refrigerator to let the frosting set and cool.
- To make the white frosting: Combine powdered sugar, vanilla, and water (if needed) in a food processor and blend until smooth. Pour frosting into a resealable plastic bag and cut off one corner of the bag. Pipe out frosting to create decorations on the fudge-frosted squares. Decorate with safe candies, edible flowers, or even try mini bows. Place each decorated treat in a mini paper muffin liner to serve.

Yield: About 3 dozen

RECIPE NOTE

Here's a fun idea: Buy a clean, unused chocolate box and mini muffin or candy paper liners from a craft store. Fill liners with decorated Petit Fours and decorate the box. This makes a wonderful present for anyone, with or without allergies. Give this safe treat box to Grandma at Christmas instead of her usual nut candies. She'll be pleased with her delicious homemade gift, and you will be pleased to know she can give your child safe kisses!

Chocolate-Covered Trail Mix Balls

½ cup (130 g) sunflower butter

¼ cup (60 ml) brown rice syrup

½ cup (75 g) Enjoy Life Not Nuts!

Beach Bash trail mix

½ cup (87 g) Enjoy Life semi-sweet
   chocolate chips (optional)

DIRECTIONS

- In a bowl, mix together the sunflower butter and brown rice syrup. Stir in trail mix.
- Form into 2-inch (5-cm) balls. Place on a baking sheet lined with aluminum foil or nonstick parchment paper. Chill in the refrigerator.
- Place chocolate chips in a microwave-proof bowl. Microwave at 30-second intervals, stirring frequently. Stir chocolate until completely melted and smooth.
- Remove balls from refrigerator. Place a BBQ skewer or a small cookie pop stick in one end of a ball. Carefully dip into the melted chocolate. Use a fork to help keep the ball on the stick. Lay the chocolate-covered ball on the lined baking sheet. Repeat with remaining balls. Refrigerate until chocolate has hardened.

Yield: 2 dozen

Go Nutless Trail Mix Bars

These cookies are easy to make and tasty to eat. No worries, there are really no nuts!

¾ cup (255 g) honey

¾ cup (195 g) sunflower butter

2 tablespoons (25 g) Spectrum
   Organic Shortening

1 teaspoon (2.3 g) ground cinnamon

7 cups (308 g) Enjoy Life Perky
   O's cereal

1 cup (165 g) packed sulfite-free dried
   fruit (raisins, apples, cranberries, or
   a combination)

½ cup (68 g) sunflower seed kernels
   (optional)

1 cup (175 g) Enjoy Life semi-sweet
   chocolate chips

DIRECTIONS

- In a microwave-proof bowl, stir together the honey, sunflower butter, shortening, and cinnamon. Microwave on high for about 1½ minutes, or until shortening has melted. Stir until smooth and set aside.
- In a large bowl, stir together the remaining ingredients. Add the honey mixture and stir.
- Dampen your hands with water and firmly press mixture into a greased 9-inch (23-cm) baking pan. Freeze for 30 minutes, or until cold and firm. Cut into bars or squares.

Yield: 2 dozen

Harvest Trail Mix Bars

1 recipe Go Nutless Trail Mix Bars
   (page 159)

1 (6 ounce) package (170 g) of your
   favorite Enjoy Life Not Nuts! trail mix

DIRECTIONS

- Follow directions above except omit the dried fruit, sunflower seeds, and chocolate chips. Substitute the trail mix (here) for the dried fruit and sunflower seeds.

Yield: 2 dozen

So Super Sopaipillas

These are golden fried pastry treats from Mexico.

FOR SOPAIPILLAS

1 1/4 cups (156 g) Bob's Red Mill white or brown rice flour or sorghum flour

1/2 cup (60 g) Bob's Red Mill tapioca flour

1/4 cup (32 g) cornstarch (contains corn; can use tapioca or arrowroot starch instead)

1 teaspoon (4.6 g) baking powder

1 teaspoon (6 g) salt

2 tablespoons (25 g) Spectrum Organic Shortening

3/4 cup (176 ml) warm water

Olive or vegetable oil for frying

FOR TOPPING

2 tablespoons (26 g) superfine, powdered, or raw sugar

1 teaspoon (2.3 g) ground cinnamon

OR

3 tablespoons (64 g) honey

1 teaspoon (2.3 g) ground cinnamon

DIRECTIONS

- To make the sopaipillas: In a food processor, combine flours, starch, baking powder, salt, and shortening. Pulse a few times until the mixture resembles fine breadcrumbs. Slowly add the water while pulsing the dough until you have a thick, sticky dough. Place dough in a large bowl and cover with plastic wrap; let sit for 1 hour.

- Divide dough in half. On a flat surface lined with nonstick parchment paper, place one dough half, then cover with more parchment paper and roll into a large square, keeping it as even and thin as possible. Cut into 2-inch (5-cm) squares.

- In a medium frying pan, heat oil over medium heat. Placea pea-size amount of dough in the hot oil; it should turn golden within 30 seconds. With metal tongs, place a few squares of dough in oil. Cook until golden on both sides, turning once. Place on a paper towel–lined plate to drain. Repeat with remaining dough.

- To make the topping: Combine sugar and cinnamon, if using, in a clean paper lunch bag. Put a few cooked squares in the bag, seal, and give a few shakes. Repeat.

- If using honey, arrange the mini sopaipillas on a plate, drizzle with honey and sprinkle with cinnamon.

Yield: 3 dozen

Choco-Loco Bites

This quick recipe makes yummy, portable brownies in a hurry.

½ cup (125 g) unsweetened applesauce

⅓ cup (80 ml) water

⅓ cup (80 ml) vegetable oil

1 tablespoon (15 ml) vanilla extract

¾ cup (65 g) unsweetened cocoa powder

1 cup (200 g) superfine sugar

1 ⅓ cups (166 g) Bob's Red Mill white rice flour

¼ teaspoon (1.5 g) salt

1 teaspoon (4.6 g) baking powder

1 ½ cups (263 g) Enjoy Life semi-sweet chocolate chips

DIRECTIONS

- Preheat oven to 350°F (180°C, or gas mark 4).
- With a mixer, beat the applesauce, water, oil, vanilla, cocoa, and sugar until smooth. Add the flour, salt, and baking powder and mix until well combined. Stir in the chocolate chips.
- Spoon batter into greased mini muffin tins. Do not over-fill.
- Bake for about 25 minutes, or until brownie is firm around the corners and leaves an indentation when poked in the middle. Let cool completely, then remove from the tin with a small knife or spatula.
- Frost or dust with powdered sugar if desired.

Yield: 2 dozen

Easy Eatin' Oat Drops

1 ³/₄ cups (350 g) superfine sugar

¹/₂ cup (120 ml) rice milk or safe milk alternative

¹/₄ cup (50 g) Spectrum Organic Shortening

¹/₂ cup (130 g) sunflower butter

1 teaspoon (5 ml) vanilla extract

3 cups (240 g) certified gluten-free rolled oats

¹/₂ cup (82 g) packed sulfite-free raisins

DIRECTIONS

• In a medium saucepan, combine sugar, rice milk, and shortening. Bring to a boil and cook for 1½ minutes. Remove from heat and mix in sunflower butter and vanilla extract. Stir in oats and raisins.

• Drop dough by teaspoonfuls onto nonstick parchment paper. Let cool until firm. Refrigerate.

Yield: 3 dozen

Marvelous Marshmallow Squares

Although not a formal "cookie," this is a good recipe to know. I cut mine into large square bars. You can eat them like a cookie! Stack them on a Oh Honey Grahams (page 164) and drizzle some chocolate on top for homemade safe S'mores! Note that this recipe contains corn ingredients.

1 ½ cups (360 ml) water, divided

4 envelopes (4 tablespoons, or 28 g) unflavored gelatin (animal or fish-free option)

3 cups (600 g) superfine sugar

¼ cup (60 ml) light corn syrup

1 teaspoon (6 g) salt

2 ½ teaspoons (12.5 ml) powdered vanilla extract

1 cup (120 g) powdered sugar (contains cornstarch; can use corn-free recipe on page 43)

DIRECTIONS

- Pour ¾ cup (180 ml) water in the bowl of a mixer. Sprinkle with gelatin; let soften for 5 minutes.
- Place the sugar, corn syrup, salt, and remaining ¾ cup (180 ml) water in a saucepan and bring to a boil for about 4 minutes (a candy thermometer should register 240°F [115°C]).
- With the mixer on low speed, carefully add hot sugar syrup to the gelatin mixture, pouring in a long, thin stream. Increase speed to high and beat until stiff peaks form, about 12 minutes. Beat in the vanilla extract.
- Pour mixture into a greased 9-inch (23-cm) glass baking dish. Let stand at room temperature for 5 hours, or until firm. Sift powdered sugar onto a cookie sheet lined with aluminum foil. Invert pan onto cookie sheet. Using an oiled knife, cut into desired size squares. Roll in or sprinkle with powdered sugar.

Yield: 3 dozen

Oh Honey Grahams

Take these cookies when you go camping and make some S'mores!

½ cup (120 ml) vegetable oil

½ cup (115 g) packed dark
   brown sugar

½ cup (170 g) honey

1 teaspoon (5 ml) vanilla extract

1 ½ cups (185 g) Bob's Red Mill
   white or brown rice flour or
   sorghum flour

1 cup (100 g) rice bran

1 cup (112 g) flax meal

1 teaspoon (4.6 g) baking powder

½ teaspoon (2.3 g) baking soda

½ teaspoon (3 g) salt

2 teaspoons (4.6 g) ground cinnamon

½ cup (120 ml) rice milk or safe
   milk alternative

Extra rice flour or bran for rolling

DIRECTIONS

- In a mixing bowl or food processor, cream together the oil, brown sugar, honey, and vanilla until fluffy. Add the flour and next 6 ingredients (through cinnamon). While mixing, slowly add in the milk.

- Divide the dough into 4 equal pieces. Roll each piece into a ball. If dough is sticky you can refrigerate until firm for about 30 minutes.

- Sprinkle some rice bran on a flat work surface. Cover a ball of dough with plastic wrap. With a rolling pin, roll out the dough into a 15-inch (37.5-cm) rectangle.

- With a knife, cut the edges into a perfect rectangle. Indent the rectangle in the center to look like two squares. Do not cut all the way through. Prick each square with a fork like a graham cracker. Repeat with remaining dough. Gently arrange rectangles on a greased cookie sheet.

- Alternatively, place all of the dough on a greased jelly roll pan, spreading out as much as possible. Put a large piece of nonstick parchment paper over the pan, and with a rolling pin roll out dough as close to the edges as possible. Make sure the dough is even in thickness. With a sharp knife score into 24 bars. Prick each square with a fork like a graham cracker.

- Bake for 15 minutes, or until lightly browned around the edges. Let cool on cookie sheet, then remove to a flat surface to cool completely. Be gentle with crackers until completely cooled.

Yield: 2 dozen

Enjoy Life Chocolate Boom Bark

A semi-sweet chocolate bar with delicious goodies on top.

12 Enjoy Life Double Chocolate
    Brownie cookies or Snickerdoodle
    cookies

1 cup (150 g) Enjoy Life Not Nuts!
Beach Bash or Mountain Mambo
trail mix

1 cup (175 g) Enjoy Life semi-sweet
    chocolate chips

DIRECTIONS

- Place all the cookies in a large resealable plastic bag and, with your hands or a rolling pin, crumble cookies into bite-size pieces. Place cookie crumbles in a large bowl. Add the trail mix and stir together.
- In a microwave-proof bowl, heat chocolate chips at 30-second intervals, stirring at each interval, until melted. Stir until smooth.
- Line and grease a 9-inch (23-cm) baking pan with aluminum foil or nonstick parchment paper. Pour the melted chocolate into the pan. Spread evenly to cover the bottom of the pan. Sprinkle cookie mixture over the melted chocolate. Press down gently. Place in the refrigerator to cool for about 30 minutes.
- Gently pull the foil or parchment paper ends up and remove chocolate block to a flat surface. Chop with a sharp knife into uneven pieces.

Yield: 2 dozen

Cookie Pizza Pizzazz!

This is great for a birthday party. Make individual cookie pizzas by scooping dough out with a large cookie scoop, flattening, and baking for 15 minutes.

FOR PIZZA

⅓ cup (80 ml) vegetable oil

½ cup (115 g) packed brown sugar

1 tablespoon (15 ml) vanilla extract

1 cup (125 g) Bob's Red Mill white rice flour

½ cup (65 g) cornstarch (contains corn; can use tapioca or arrowroot starch instead)

1 teaspoon (4.6 g) baking powder

¼ cup (60 ml) plus 2 tablespoons (30 ml) water

FOR FROSTING

2 cups (240 g) powdered sugar (contains cornstarch; can use corn-free recipe on page 43)

½ cup (100 g) Spectrum Organic Shortening

1 teaspoon (5 ml) vanilla extract

3 tablespoons (45 ml) rice milk or safe milk alternative

FOR TOPPING

6 strawberries, sliced

1 cup (175 g) Enjoy Life semi-sweet chocolate chips

DIRECTIONS

- Preheat oven to 350°F (180°C, or gas mark 4).
- To make the pizza: Mix the oil, brown sugar, and vanilla. Add the flour, starch, and baking powder and mix on low speed. With mixer on low, slowly pour in the water until the dough is smooth.
- With a spatula spread dough on a greased pizza pan. Form a thicker lip around the edge of the pan, like a pizza crust.
- Bake for about 30 to 35 minutes, or until golden around the edges and soft in the center. Let cool.
- To make the frosting: Place frosting ingredients in food processor and purée until smooth and thick. Add more milk if needed. Spread frosting over the cooled cookie to within 1 inch (2.5 cm) of the edge.
- Decorate with sliced strawberries and chocolate chips or other allergy-friendly toppings. Cut into pizza wedges.

Yield: 18 slices

Carrot Cake Mini Marvels

FOR CAKES

1 cup (225 g) packed brown sugar

1 cup (200 g) granulated sugar

$1/2$ cup (125 g) applesauce

$1/2$ cup (120 ml) vegetable oil

$1/4$ cup (28 g) flax meal

1 teaspoon (5 ml) pure vanilla extract

$1 1/2$ cups (185 g) Bob's Red Mill white or brown rice flour

$1/2$ cup (60 g) Bob's Red Mill tapioca flour

1 teaspoon (4.6 g) baking soda

1 teaspoon (4.6 g) baking powder

$1/4$ teaspoon (1.5 g) salt

1 teaspoon (2. 3 g) ground cinnamon

$1/2$ teaspoon (1.1 g) ground nutmeg

$1/2$ teaspoon (0.9 g) ground ginger

2 cups (160 g) certified gluten-free rolled oats

$1 1/2$ cups (180 g) finely grated carrots (about 3 large carrots)

1 cup (165 g) packed sulfite-free raisins

FOR FILLING

2 cups (240 g) powdered sugar (contains cornstarch; can use corn-free recipe on page 43)

2 tablespoons (25 g) Spectrum Organic Shortening

2 tablespoons (30 ml) rice milk or safe milk alternative

$1/2$ teaspoon (2.5 ml) vanilla extract

Dash of salt

DIRECTIONS

- Preheat oven to 350°F (180°C, or gas mark 4).
- For the cakes: In a mixer cream together sugars, applesauce, oil, flax, and vanilla. Add in rice flour and next 7 ingredients (through ginger) and blend until smooth. Mix in oats, carrots, and raisins. Chill dough in fridge until firm, at least 1 hour.
- Using a small ice cream/cookie scoop, scoop dough onto a baking sheet lined with nonstick parchment paper or aluminum foil, leaving 2 inches (5 cm) between cookies. Flatten slightly.
- Bake for 15 minutes, or until golden. Remove with a spatula to a flat surface to cool.
- For filling: Combine filling ingredients in a food processor and pulse until smooth.
- Once cookies have cooled completely, use a spatula to spread about 2 teaspoons of filling onto a cookie. Top with a second cookie to make a sandwich. Repeat with remaining cookies.

Yield: 2 dozen

Mini' nana Fries

*These are a popular treat in Southeast Asia. Dipped in a cookie batter,
these tiny finger-size treats will please the whole family. You can also use
pineapple rings or apple wedges, if desired.*

10 Enjoy Life Snickerdoodle cookies

2 teaspoons (5 g) Bob's Red Mill
   tapioca flour

1/2 teaspoon (2.3 g) baking powder

2 teaspoons (14 g) honey

1 teaspoon (2.3 g) ground cinnamon

2/3 cup (160 ml) water

6 firm bananas

1/2 cup (120 ml) vegetable oil

1/2 cup (60 g) white rice flour

Vegetable oil for frying

DIRECTIONS

- Place cookies in a food processor and pulse until mixture resembles cornmeal. Add the flour and next 4 ingredients (through water). Purée until you have a smooth, thin batter. Pour into a bowl and set aside.
- Peel bananas and cut off the ends. Slice bananas lengthwisedown the center and then into halves. You should have 4 even pieces from each banana. Place rice flour in a shallow bowl and coat each banana piece with flour. Shake and set aside.
- Line a plate with nonstick parchment paper or a clean, unused brown paper bag. Set aside.
- Heat oil in a small frying pan over medium-low heat. The temperature is correct when a pea-size drop of batter sizzles and turns golden within 15 seconds. Remove with a fork or slotted metal spatula.
- Coat one banana at a time in the cookie batter. Gently place one coated banana in the hot oil. It should start to get golden in about 10 seconds. Use a fork or spatula and gently roll the banana to the other side, letting the banana cook until golden all over. If the batter gets too dark, remove the banana and turn the heat down. Carefully remove the banana with a fork or spatula to the prepared plate to drain. Repeat with remaining bananas, one or two at a time.
- Dab each banana with a paper towel to soak up excess oil. Serve right away.

Yield: 2 dozen

Chocolate-Covered Bananas

2 bananas

1/2 cup (85 g) Enjoy Life semi-sweet
   chocolate chips

4 Popsicle sticks or cookie dowels

DIRECTIONS

- Peel bananas and cut each in half across the middle (you will have 4 banana pieces total). Insert a wooden stick into the flat end of each banana half. Lay bananas in a shallow pan lined with aluminum foil and freeze for about 3 hours.
- Place chocolate chips in a microwave-safe bowl. Heat in 30-second intervals, stirring at each interval, until melted. Stir until smooth.
- Drizzle chocolate over bananas, or dip the frozen bananas into the bowl of warm chocolate. Place back onto the lined pan and freeze until chocolate hardens.

Yield: 4 pieces

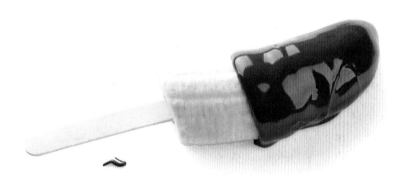

Fruit Coulis Rice Bars

This treat is traditionally made with coconut milk and is commonly served in countries all over the Far East along with tropical fruits like mangoes or pineapples. Here I modify it with fresh raspberries and omit the coconut. This isn't a bar cookie that you can eat with your hands, but it is a very delicious and unique treat.

FOR BARS

1/2 cup (100 g) jasmine rice, soaked overnight in 3/4 cup (180 ml) water

2 cups (475 ml) rice milk or safe milk alternative

1/4 cup (50 g) superfine sugar

FOR FRUIT COULIS

3/4 cup (110 g) fresh raspberries or blackberries

2 tablespoons (26 g) superfine sugar

DIRECTIONS

- To make the bars: Place rice and the soaking water into a food processor and process for a few minutes until the mixture is soupy.
- Heat the rice milk in a saucepan. Bring to a boil and stir in rice mixture. Cook over very low heat for 10 minutes, stirring constantly.
- Stir in the sugar and continue cooking for an additional 15 minutes, or until thick and creamy.
- Line a 9 x 13-inch (23 x 33-cm) baking pan with aluminum foil or nonstick parchment paper. Pour rice mixture into the pan, cool, and then chill in the refrigerator until the dessert is set and firm.
- To make the fruit coulis: Place berries and sugar in a food processor. Pulse until well combined.
- Cut the chilled rice into small bars. To serve, spoon a little coulis over each rice bar on a plate. Decorate with additional fresh berries if desired.

Yield: 2 dozen

Rocky Road Bites

A fudgy bite full of yummy goodies.

1 ½ cups (168 g, or about 12 cookies) Enjoy Life Snickerdoodle cookies or Double Chocolate Brownie cookies, crumbled into pieces

1 ¼ cups (63 g) safe miniature marshmallows

¼ cup (34 g) salted sunflower seed or (57 g) pumpkin seed kernels

2 cups (350 g) Enjoy Life semi-sweet chocolate chips

2 tablespoons (25 g) Spectrum Organic Shortening

¾ cup (90 g) powdered sugar (contains cornstarch; can use corn-free recipe on page 43)

2 to 3 tablespoons (30 to 45 ml) rice milk or safe milk alternative

DIRECTIONS

- In a large bowl, combine cookie crumbs, marshmallows, and seeds. Set aside.
- Place chocolate chips in a microwave-safe bowl. Heat in 30-second intervals, stirring at each interval, until melted. Stir until smooth. Add in the shortening and stir until melted and mixture cools down a bit, but is still easy to stir. When mixture has cooled slightly, stir in the powdered sugar and rice milk. Mixture will thicken like fudge.
- Add chocolate mixture to the cookie mixture. Stir briefly until well coated.
- Line and grease a 9-inch (23-cm) baking pan with aluminum foil or nonstick parchment paper. Pour the batter into the pan. Spread evenly to cover the bottom of the pan. Place in the refrigerator to chill until set.
- Gently pull the foil or nonstick parchment paper ends up and remove chocolate block to a flat surface. Use a sharp knife to cut into small squares.

Yield: 2 dozen

Toasty Cinnamon Treats

These were one of my favorite hand-held treats when I was little. With my kids I use fun cookie cutters to make little treats, and I munch on the end pieces! You can replace the oil with sunflower butter for a heartier snack.

4 pieces safe bread

1 tablespoon (13 g) raw sugar

1 teaspoon (2.6 g) ground cinnamon

2 tablespoons (30 ml) olive, canola, or vegetable oil

DIRECTIONS

- Preheat oven to broil.
- Lay the bread on a flat, clean surface. Mix together sugar and cinnamon in a small bowl. Place oil in a seperate bowl.
- Dip a pastry brush in the oil and coat each piece of bread. Generously sprinkle sugar mixture over the the oiled bread.
- Use small cookie cutters to cut shapes out of the bread, using as much of the bread as possible. If you do not have cookie cutters, use a small drinking glass turned upside down to use as a cookie cutter, or cut bread into finger-size sticks.
- Place shapes on a greased baking sheet.
- Broil for about 7 minutes. You may need to move toast around the baking sheet for even toasting. Remove to a flat surface to cool. Serve warm or at room temperature.

Yield: 12 pieces

Pancakes are not your typical cookie, but they **are** some of kids' favorite foods! I jazzed up your average pancake to make it more like a treat. Syrup is an option with these guys, but they're great if you just want to grab one on the go.

Mini-ficent Pancakes

1 cup (125 g) Bob's Red Mill white or brown rice flour

1 tablespoon (13 g) superfine sugar or (21 g) honey

2 teaspoons (9.2 g) baking powder

⅓ cup (43 g) cornstarch (contains corn; can use tapioca or arrowroot starch instead) or tapioca flour

¾ cup (180 ml) rice milk, safe milk alternative, or water

3 tablespoons (45 ml) vegetable oil

Dash of salt

DIRECTIONS

- In a large bowl, whisk together all ingredients.
- Heat a greased skillet. Drop a pea-size amount of batter in skillet; skillet is at correct temperature when batter turns golden quickly. Remove batter piece with a spatula. Pour ¼ cup (60 ml) of batter into skillet. When air bubbles form on the top, flip over with a flat spatula. Cook on the other side and remove to a plate. You may cook 3 to 4 cakes at a time depending on the size of the skillet.
- Sprinkle with powdered sugar or serve with a small cup of natural syrup, honey, unsweetened applesauce, or jam.

Yield: 2 dozen

Amply Apple Pancakes

1 ½ cups (185 g) Bob's Red Mill brown or white rice flour or sorghum flour

1 tablespoon (13 g) superfine sugar or (21 g) honey

2 teaspoons (9.2 g) baking powder

2 tablespoons (16 g) cornstarch (contains corn; can use tapioca or arrowroot starch instead) or tapioca flour

½ cup (120 ml) rice milk, safe milk alternative, or water

½ cup (125 g) unsweetened applesauce

1 teaspoon (2.3 g) ground cinnamon

Dash of salt

2 tablespoons (30 ml) vegetable oil

1 small apple, chopped into almond-size pieces

DIRECTIONS

- In a large bowl, whisk together all ingredients except apples. Stir in apple pieces.
- Heat a greased skillet. Drop a pea-size amount of batter in skillet; skillet is as correct temperature when batter turns golden quickly. Remove batter piece with a spatula. Pour ¼ cup (60 ml) of batter into skillet. When air bubbles form on the top, flip over with a flat spatula. Cook on the other side and remove to a plate. You may cook 3 to 4 cakes at a time depending on the size of the skillet.
- Sprinkle with powdered sugar or cinnamon or serve with a small cup of natural syrup, honey, unsweetened applesauce, or jam.

Yield: 2 dozen

Chocolate-Lovers' Pancakes

1 cup (125 g) Bob's Red Mill white or brown rice flour

1 tablespoon (13 g) superfine sugar or (21 g) honey

2 teaspoons (9.2 g) baking powder

⅓ cup (43 g) cornstarch (contains corn; can use tapioca or arrowroot starch instead) or tapioca flour

¾ cup (180 ml) rice milk, safe milk alternative, or water

3 tablespoons (45 ml) vegetable oil

Dash of salt

½ cup (87 g) Enjoy Life semi-sweet chocolate chips

Powdered sugar or cinnamon (optional)

DIRECTIONS

- In a large bowl, whisk together flour, sugar, baking powder, starch, rice milk, oil, and salt. Stir in chocolate chips.
- Heat a greased skillet. Drop a pea-size amount of batter in skillet; skillet is at correct temperature when batter turns golden quickly. Remove batter piece with a spatula. Pour ¼ cup (60 ml) of batter into skillet. When air bubbles form on the top, flip over with a spatula. Cook on the other side and remove to a plate. You may cook 3 to 4 cakes at a time depending on the size of the skillet.
- Sprinkle with powdered sugar or cinnamon, if desired.

Yield: 2 dozen

Berry Yummy Pancakes

1 cup (125 g) Bob's Red Mill white or brown rice flour

1 tablespoon (13 g) superfine sugar or (21 g) honey

2 teaspoons (9.2 g) baking powder

⅓ cup (43 g) cornstarch (contains corn; can use tapioca or arrowroot starch instead) or tapioca flour

¾ cup (180 ml) rice milk, safe milk alternative, or water

3 tablespoons (45 ml) vegetable oil

Dash of salt

1 teaspoon (2.3 g) ground cinnamon or (1.7 g) lemon zest

1 cup (145 g) small fresh blueberries

Powdered sugar (optional)

DIRECTIONS

- In a large bowl, whisk together flour, sugar, baking powder, starch, rice milk, oil, salt, and cinnamon or zest. Stir in blueberries.
- Heat a greased skillet. Drop a pea-size amount of batter in skillet; skillet is at correct temperature when batter turns golden quickly. Remove batter piece with a spatula. Pour ¼ cup (60 ml) of batter into skillet. When air bubbles form on the top, flip over with a flat spatula. Cook on the other side and remove to a plate. You may cook 3 to 4 cakes at a time depending on the size of the skillet.
- Sprinkle with powdered sugar, if desired.

Yield: 2 dozen

Gingerbread Man Pancakes

1 ¼ cups (155 g) Bob's Red Mill white or brown rice flour

¼ cup (28 g) flax meal

2 tablespoons (30 ml) unsulfured molasses

1 tablespoon (15 g) packed brown sugar or (21 g) honey

2 teaspoons (9.2 g) baking powder

¼ teaspoon (1.2 g) baking soda

1 teaspoon (5 ml) distilled vinegar

2 tablespoons (16 g) cornstarch (contains corn; can use tapioca or arrowroot starch instead)

1 ¼ cups (285 ml) rice milk or safe milk beverage alternative or water

2 tablespoons (30 ml) vegetable oil

¼ teaspoon (1.5 g) salt

1 teaspoon (2.3 g) ground cinnamon or pumpkin pie spice (or make your own; see page 42)

Powdered sugar (optional)

DIRECTIONS

- In a large bowl, whisk together all ingredients except powdered sugar.
- Heat a greased skillet. Drop a pea-size amount of batter in skillet; skillet is at correct temperature when batter turns golden quickly. Remove batter piece with a spatula. Pour ¼ cup (60 ml) of batter into skillet. When air bubbles form on the top, flip over with a flat spatula. Cook on the other side and remove to a plate. You may cook 3 to 4 pancakes at a time depending on the size of the skillet.
- Sprinkle with powdered sugar, if desired.

Yield: 2 dozen

Sunshine Crepes

FOR CREPES

³/₄ cup (94 g) Bob's Red Mill white or brown rice flour

¹/₄ cup (32 g) cornstarch (contains corn; can use tapioca or arrowroot starch instead)

1 teaspoon (4.6 g) baking powder

¹/₂ teaspoon (3 g) salt

2 tablespoons (16 g) powdered sugar (contains cornstarch; can use corn-free recipe on page 43)

²/₃ cup (160 ml) rice milk or safe milk alternative

¹/₃ cup (80 ml) water

1 teaspoon (5 ml) vanilla extract

2 tablespoons (30 ml) olive oil

FOR FILLING

1 tablespoon (15 ml) vegetable oil

2 tablespoons (30 g) packed brown sugar

2 apples, peaches, or bananas, thinly sliced or 1 ¹/₂ cups (180 g) fresh fruit, such as blueberries, cherries, raspberries, or strawberries

Dash of ground cinnamon (optional)

DIRECTIONS

- To make the crepes: Combine all crepe ingredients in a bowl and stir until just combined. Batter will be a little lumpy. Let sit for 30 minutes to 1 hour, or make the night before and let it sit in the refrigerator in a sealed container.
- Grease a crepe pan or small frying pan and preheat over medium-high heat. Pour ¹/₄ cup (60 ml) batter into pan. Swirl the mixture in pan until the batter covers the bottom. It will start to bubble right away. Let cook for less than 30 seconds. Use a plastic spatula to flip over and cook for about 15 seconds on the other side. Remove to a plate. Repeat with remaining batter. You may need to grease the pan before cooking each crepe to prevent sticking.
- Let crepes sit for 15 minutes. They are more pliable and easier to roll after they cool.
- To make the filling: In the crepe pan, cook the oil and brown sugar until melted. Add the fruit and sauté until tender. Stir in the cinnamon, if desired.
- To serve, spoon some filling over the middle of crepe. Roll it around the filling. Top with powdered sugar, reserved filling, or serve plain.

Yield: 16 crepes

'Frigerator Fudge

9 ounces (255 g) Enjoy Life semi-
  sweet chocolate chips

2 tablespoons (25 g) Spectrum
  Organic Shortening

¼ cup (60 ml) rice milk or safe
  milk alternative

3 cups (360 g) powdered sugar
  (contains cornstarch; can use
  corn-free recipe on page 43)

DIRECTIONS

- In a large microwave-safe bowl, combine chocolate chips, shortening, and milk.
  Microwave in 30-second intervals, stirring at each interval, until melted. Stir
  quickly until smooth. Whisk in the powdered sugar.

- Press chocolate mixture into a greased 8-inch (20-cm) square baking pan. Chill
  in the refrigerator until firm, about 2 hours. Loosen the edges by running a flat
  spatula or knife around the edges. Use a sharp knife to cut into squares. Sift
  powdered sugar over top, if desired.

Yield: 2 dozen squares

Apple Fritter Critters

These are like a combination of an apple cookie and a donut.

FOR FRITTERS

¼ cup (28 g) flax meal

⅔ cup (160 ml) plus 1 tablespoon
 (15 ml) rice milk or safe milk
 alternative

2 tablespoons (30 ml) vegetable oil

1 tablespoon (13 g) superfine sugar

⅓ cup (42 g) Bob's Red Mill
 tapioca flour

1 ⅔ cups (208 g) Bob's Red Mill
 white or brown rice flour or
 sorghum flour

1 teaspoon (6 g) salt

1 tablespoon (13.8 g) baking powder

½ teaspoon (1.2 g) ground cinnamon

1 cup (150 g) chopped apple (about
 1 medium apple)

Vegetable oil for frying

FOR TOPPING

1 cup (120 g) powdered sugar
 (contains cornstarch; can use
 corn-free recipe on page 43)

OR

½ cup (100 g) superfine sugar

1 teaspoon (2.3 g) ground cinnamon

DIRECTIONS

- To make the fritters: In a bowl, mix together all fritter ingredients except oil.
- Heat oil in a frying pan over medium heat. Place a pea-size amount of batter in oil; oil is the correct temperature if the batter browns fairly quickly. Lower the heat of the frying pan if necessary. Remove batter piece.
- Line a plate with paper towels. With a small ice cream/cookie scoop or a ¼ cup (60 ml) metal measuring cup, drop batter into oil. Cook until bottom is golden, then use a metal fork or spatula to flip the fritter over and cook until golden all over.
- Remove from pan and place on plate to cool. Repeat with remaining batter. (Hint: Cut the first fritter in half to make sure it is cooked all the way through to help you judge how long the cooking time should be on each side.)
- To make the topping: Place powdered sugar or sugar and cinnamon in a bag. Place 2 to 3 fritters in the bag, roll the bag closed, and gently shake to coat. Repeat with remaining fritters. Store fritters in a clean paper bag, sealed.

Yield: 2 dozen

Applicious Empanadas

These little mini pies are inspired by Mexican treats.

FOR DOUGH

1 ½ cups (185 g) Bob's Red Mill
    sorghum flour

¼ cup (60 ml) vegetable oil

¼ teaspoon (1.5 g) salt

¼ cup (60 ml) pure maple syrup

¼ cup (28 g) flax meal

⅓ cup (43 g) cornstarch (contains
    corn; can use tapioca or arrowroot
    starch instead)

FOR APPLE FILLING

2 tablespoons (30 ml) vegetable oil

½ cup (115 g) packed brown sugar

2 tablespoons (30 ml) water

3 apples or pears (or a combination),
    cut into almond-size pieces

¼ cup (40 g) packed sulfite-free
    raisins

DIRECTIONS

- Preheat oven to 350°F (180°C, or gas mark 4).
- To make the dough: Place all dough ingredients in a food processor. Pulse until you have a firm dough that forms a ball. If mixture is too dry and does not form into a ball, add water 1 teaspoon (5 ml) at a time. Let dough sit for 10 minutes.
- To make filling: Heat the oil, sugar, and water in a saucepan until dissolved and thick. Add the apples and raisins. Sauté until apples are tender. Set aside to cool.
- Pinch off a piece of dough the size of a golf ball. Roll into a flat disk or circle, about ⅛ inch (30 mm) thick. You may place dough between two pieces of nonstick parchment paper to make rolling easier.
- Place 1 tablespoon (20g) of filling on one half of the dough circle. With a flat spatula, flip the other half of the dough over to make a half circle with one rounded side and one flat side. Press the tines of a fork into the dough on the rounded side to seal. Brush the tops of the empanadas with water. Sprinkle raw sugar over the tops, if desired. Place about 8 empanadas on a greased baking sheet.
- Bake for about 15 to 20 minutes, or until edges are golden. Remove from the baking sheet immediately with a spatula to a flat surface to cool. Empanadas are good warm or at room temperature.

Yield: 16 empanadas

Flight-of-Fancy Florentines

Traditional florentines are a delicious mixture of toasted nuts and candied fruit coated with a sweet and sticky mixture of honey and sugar and baked until golden brown and bubbly. The crowning touch is a layer of melted chocolate. Try this allergy-friendly version in a bar form.

FOR BASE

½ cup (100 g) superfine sugar

½ cup (170 g) honey

2 cups (300 g) Enjoy Life Not Nuts! Mountain Mambo or Beach Bash trail mix

⅓ cup (42 g) Bob's Red Mill white rice flour

¼ teaspoon (0.5 g) ground allspice (optional)

¼ teaspoon (0.6 g) freshly grated nutmeg (optional)

FOR CHOCOLATE TOPPING

3 ounces (85 g) Enjoy Life semi-sweet chocolate chips

1 teaspoon (5 ml) vegetable oil or (4 g) Spectrum Organic Shortening

DIRECTIONS

- Preheat oven to 350°F (180°C, or gas mark 4).
- To make the base: In a small saucepan, warm the sugar and honey over low heat until the sugar has completely dissolved. Stir in remaining base ingredients. Spread mixture into a greased 9-inch (23-cm) square baking pan, smoothing the top evenly.
- Bake for 25 to 30 minutes or until golden brown and bubbly. Remove from oven and set aside to cool.
- To make the cocolate topping: Melt the chocolate chips and oil in a microwave-safe bowl at medium heat in 30-second intervals, stirring at each interval, until melted and smooth. Stir well. Spread the melted chocolate over the completely cooled Florentine and let cool before cutting into small bars.

Yield: 2 dozen

Amazing No-Bake Cinnamon Rolls

5 prepared crepes or plain pancakes, cooled (see pages 173, 178)

2 tablespoons (30 ml) vegetable oil

2 tablespoons (26 g) superfine sugar

2 tablespoons (14 g) ground cinnamon

2 tablespoons (16 g) powdered sugar (contains cornstarch; can use corn-free recipe on page 43)

¼ teaspoon (1.3 ml) vanilla extract

DIRECTIONS

- With a pastry brush, brush oil on one side of each crepe.
- In a small bowl, mix the sugar and cinnamon. Sprinkle mixture over the oiled crepes. Roll into a wrap. You can brush more oil on the edges to help seal, if needed.
- Cut each wrap into pieces and lay flat with cinnamon swirls showing.
- Mix together powdered sugar and vanilla. Add a drop of water if needed to achieve a good consistency for drizzling. With a spoon, drizzle powdered sugar mixture over the tops of the rolls. Sprinkle with cinnamon, if desired. Serve immediately.

Yield: 20 rolls

Bravo Brownie Cut-Ups

*These are super-easy and fun. My kids love using the cookie cutters
to make star brownies.*

- 1 cup (200 g) superfine sugar
- 1/3 cup (42 g) Bob's Red Mill tapioca flour
- 1/3 cup (42 g) Bob's Red Mill white rice flour
- 1/2 cup (43 g) unsweetened cocoa
- 1/2 cup (125 g) unsweetened applesauce
- 1/4 cup (60 ml) water
- 1 teaspoon (5 ml) vanilla extract
- 1/2 teaspoon (2.3 g) baking powder
- 1/4 cup (30 g) powdered sugar (contains cornstarch; can use corn-free recipe on page 43)

DIRECTIONS

- Preheat oven to 350°F (180°C, or gas mark 4).
- With a mixer, blend all ingredients except powdered sugar until smooth. Line an 8-inch (20-cm) square baking pan with aluminum foil, extending foil over sides of pan. Pour batter into pan.
- Bake for 30 minutes, or until edges are firm.
- Cool completely in pan. Place in freezer for 15 minutes for easier cutting. Lift brownies from pan using sides of foil; carefully peel off foil.
- Cut into squares or other desired shapes with small cookie cutters. Sift powdered sugar over tops of brownies.

Yield: About 16 brownies

Crunchkins

5 teaspoons (25 ml) vegetable oil

1 package (10 ounce, or 280 g) safe marshmallows (contains corn ingredients)

1 teaspoon (5 ml) vanilla extract

6 cups (265 g) safe cereal of your choice, such as Enjoy Life Perky O's cereal

DIRECTIONS

- In a large, microwave safe bowl, mix together the oil and marshmallows. Microwave on high for about two minutes, or just until the marshmallows begin to puff up.
- Remove from the microwave and stir until mixture is smooth (you may have to microwave a bit longer after stirring). Stir in the vanilla. Add the cereal and stir until cereal is evenly coated with the marshmallow mixture.
- Moisten your hands with water to prevent the mixture from sticking. Using your hands, roll the cereal mixture into balls. Repeat with remaining mixture. Chill in the refrigerator until set.

Yield: 2 dozen

Gimme S'more Bites

Delicious.

1 (1.4-ounce, 40-g) Enjoy Life boom CHOCO boom dark chocolate or dairy-free rice milk bar

8 Enjoy Life Snickerdoodle or Double Chocolate Brownie cookies

4 large safe marshmallows (see page 163)

DIRECTIONS

- Divide candy bar into 4 pieces.
- Slightly flatten 4 cookies.
- On a microwave-safe plate, place one slightly flattened cookie and top with a chocolate piece. Gently press a marshmallow on top of the chocolate piece. Place a non-flattened cookie on top of the marshmallow. Microwave on low heat for 15 seconds or until chocolate and marshmallow are slightly soft. You may drizzle additional melted chocolate over the cookie, if desired. Eat immediately.

Yield: 4 cookies

Chocolate Sunflower Truffles

6 ounces (170 g) Enjoy Life semi-sweet chocolate chips

3 tablespoons (37.5 g) Spectrum Organic Shortening

2 tablespoons (30 ml) rice milk or safe milk alternative

3 ½ tablespoons (28 g) powdered sugar (contains cornstarch; can use corn free recipe on page 43)

½ cup (112 g) sunflower seed kernels, ground into a meal

1 (1.4-ounce, 40-g) Enjoy Life boom CHOCO boom dark chocolate or dairy-free rice milk bar, grated

DIRECTIONS

- Place chocolate chips in a microwave-safe bowl and heat in 30-second intervals, stirring at each interval until smooth. Stir in the shortening, milk, powdered sugar, and ground sunflower seeds. Let sit to cool until firm enough to roll into balls.
- Place the grated chocolate on a rimmed plate and roll the truffles in the grated chocolate to coat them. Place the truffles in mini cupcake liners and chill in the refrigerator.

Yield: 2 dozen

Yummy Sunny Day Fudge

2 1/4 cups (450 g) superfine sugar

1 3/4 cups (87.5 g) safe mini marshmallows

1/3 cup (80 ml) rice milk or safe milk alternative

3/4 cup (180 ml) hot water

1/4 cup (50 g) Spectrum Organic Shortening or (60 ml) vegetable oil

1 teaspoon (5 ml) vanilla extract

1/2 cup (130 g) sunflower butter

1 cup (175 g) Enjoy Life semi-sweet chocolate chips

DIRECTIONS

- Combine the sugar, marshmallows, rice milk, water, and oil in a saucepan. Cook over medium heat, stirring constantly, until the mixture boils. Cook an additional 5 minutes.
- While sugar mixture is cooking, place the sunflower butter in a medium bowl and the chocolate chips into another medium bowl.
- Remove saucepan from heat and add the vanilla. Immediately pour half of the hot mixture into the bowl with the sunflower butter and mix until smooth. Pour sunflower butter mixture into an 8-inch (20-cm) square pan lined with aluminum foil.
- Stir the remaining marshmallow mixture into the bowl with the chocolate chips. Stir until the chocolate chips are melted and mixture is smooth. Immediately spread over the sunflower butter layer.
- Chill in the refrigerator until fudge is completely cooled. Remove from the pan and place the fudge on a cutting board. Remove the foil. Cut into 1½-inch (3.7-cm) squares. Dust with powdered sugar, if desired.

Yield: 2 dozen

Yum in a Haystack

Why is it that salty crunchiness and sweet chocolate makes for the best stress relief?
Don't just make these for the kids; they are good treats for parents too!

½ cup (85 g) Enjoy Life semi-sweet
   chocolate chips

1 teaspoon (4 g) Spectrum
   Organic Shortening

2 teaspoons (10 ml) rice milk or safe
   milk alternative

½ cup (75 g) Enjoy Life Not Nuts!
   Beach Mambo trail mix

¼ cup (18 g) Enjoy Life Perky O's
   cereal or safe rice flakes cereal,
   crushed (optional)

DIRECTIONS

- In a small saucepan over medium heat, stir together chocolate chips, shortening, and rice milk until melted and smooth, about 1 minute. Remove from heat and stir in trail mix and crushed cereal.
- Drop tablespoons of chocolate mixture onto aluminum foil or nonstick parchment paper. With a spoon, shape the mixture into clusters.
- Chill completely in the refrigerator before serving. Refrigerate leftovers on a covered plate.

Yield: 2 dozen

Mountain Mambo Biscotti

*This crunchy biscotti has a wonderful flavor and is perfect with
a cup of hot tea or cocoa.*

¼ cup (60 ml) light olive oil or
   vegetable oil

¾ cup (150 g) sugar

2 teaspoons (10 ml) vanilla extract

¼ cup (60 g) unsweetened
   applesauce

¼ cup (28 g) flax meal

2 tablespoons (30 ml) water

½ cup (60 g) Bob's Red Mill white
   or brown rice flour

½ cup (60 g) Bob's Red Mill
   tapioca flour

¾ cup (90 g) oat or sorghum flour

¼ teaspoon (1.5 g) salt

1 teaspoon (4.6 g) baking powder

1 cup (150 g) Enjoy Life Not Nuts!
   Mountain Mambo trail mix

DIRECTIONS

- Preheat oven to 350°F (180°C, or gas mark 4).
- With a mixer, combine oil, sugar, vanilla, applesauce, flax, and water and blend. Add rice flour and next 4 ingredients (through baking powder) and mix on medium speed for about 1 minute.
- In a food processor, pulse the trail mix a few times to achieve a mealy/crumbly texture. Stir the trail mix into the dough by hand.
- Divide dough in half. Form two logs (12 x 2 inches, 30 x 5 cm) on a cookie sheet lined with nonstick parchment paper or aluminum foil.
- Bake for 30 to 35 minutes, or until logs are light brown around the edges. Remove from oven and set aside to cool for 10 minutes. Reduce oven heat to 300°F (150°C, or gas mark 2).
- Cut logs on the diagonal into ¾-inch (1.9-cm) thick slices. Lay on sides on parchment-covered baking sheet. Bake for approximately 8 minutes on one side, then turn over and bake for 5 minutes on the other side, or until dry and crunchy. Let cool.

Yield: 16 biscotti

Gingerly Ginger Biscotti

This is a really easy way to make a flavorful crunchy cookie for the holidays.

FOR BISCOTTI

⅓ cup (80 ml) vegetable oil

1 cup (200 g) superfine sugar

¼ cup (60 ml) unsulfured molasses

½ cup (125 g) unsweetened
   applesauce

1 ⅔ cups (210 g) Bob's Red Mill white
   or brown rice flour

1 cup (125 g) Bob's Red Mill
   tapioca flour

½ cup (56 g) flax meal

1 cup (100 g) rice bran

1 tablespoon (13.8 g) baking powder

1 tablespoon (5.5 g) ground ginger

1 tablespoon (7 g) ground cinnamon

1 ½ teaspoon (3.3 g) ground cloves

¼ teaspoon (0.6 g) ground nutmeg

FOR ICING

1 cup (120 g) powdered sugar
   (contains cornstarch; can use
   corn-free recipe on page 43)

Dash of ground cinnamon

1 tablespoon (15 ml) rice milk or safe
   milk alternative

DIRECTIONS

• Preheat oven to 325°F (170°C, or gas mark 3).

• To make the biscotti: In a large bowl, mix together oil, sugar, and molasses.

• In another bowl, combine remaining biscotti ingredients. Add the molasses mixture and mix well. With a small ice cream/cookie scoop drop dough on a greased baking sheet.

• Bake for 25 minutes. Let cool for 2 minutes, then remove to a flat surface to cool completely.

• To make the icing: Combine all icing ingredients in a bowl and whisk until smooth. Drizzle icing over biscotti.

Yield: 2 dozen

Frosted Tea Cakes

This is a great treat for a kid's party.

FOR CAKES

1/2 cup (100 g) Spectrum
Organic Shortening

1/2 cup (100 g) superfine sugar

1/2 cup (125 g) unsweetened
applesauce

1 teaspoon (5 ml) vanilla extract

Zest of 1 large lemon

1 1/4 cups (155 g) Bob's Red Mill white
rice flour

1 cup (125 g) Bob's Red Mill tapioca
flour or millet flour

2 teaspoons (9.2 g) baking powder

1/4 teaspoon (1.5 g) salt

FOR FROSTING

2 cups (200 g) powdered sugar
(contains cornstarch; can use
corn-free recipe on page 43)

1/2 cup (100 g) Spectrum
Organic Shortening

1 teaspoon (5 ml) vanilla extract

2 tablespoons (30 ml) rice milk
or safe milk alternative

DIRECTIONS

- Preheat oven to 350°F (180°C, or gas mark 4).
- To make the cakes: Cream together shortening, sugar, applesauce, vanilla, and zest. Add the remaining cake ingredients and mix for 1 minute.
- Line a mini muffin pan with paper liners. With a small ice cream/cookie scoop, place a scoop of dough in each lined muffin cup.
- Bake for about 20 minutes. Let cool.
- To make the frosting: In a food processor combine all frosting ingredients. Frost or decorate each mini cake.

Yield: 3 dozen

Ginger Spice Mini Scones

FOR SCONES

3 tablespoons (45 ml) unsulfured
  molasses

1 teaspoon (5 ml) vanilla extract

1/4 cup (50 g) Spectrum Organic
  Shortening

1/3 cup (75 g) packed brown sugar

1/4 cup (60 g) unsweetened
  applesauce

1 teaspoon (5 ml) distilled vinegar

1/2 cup (120 ml) rice milk or safe milk
  alternative

3/4 cup (60 g) certified gluten-free
  rolled oats, divided

1 cup (125 g) Bob's Red Mill white or
  brown rice flour

1/2 cup (56 g) flax meal

1/4 cup (30 g) Bob's Red Mill
  tapioca flour

2 teaspoons (3.6 g) ground ginger

1 1/2 teaspoons (3.5 g) ground
  cinnamon

1/8 teaspoon (0.3 g) ground cloves
  (optional)

1/4 teaspoon (1.5 g) salt

2 teaspoons (9.2 g) baking powder

1/2 teaspoon (2.3 g) baking soda

1/2 cup (75 g) dried cranberries

FOR MAPLE GLAZE

1/2 cup (50 g) powdered sugar
  (contains cornstarch; can use corn
  free recipe on page 43)

1 1/2 tablespoons (22 ml) pure
  maple syrup

1 to 2 teaspoons (5 to 10 ml) rice milk
  or safe milk beverage alternative

DIRECTIONS

- Preheat oven to 400°F (200°C, or gas mark 6).
- To make scones: Cream together molasses, vanilla, shortening, brown sugar, apple-
  sauce, vinegar, and milk with a mixer. Add 1/2 cup plus 1 tablespoon (45 g) oats and
  next nine ingredients and blend well. Stir in cranberries.
- Using a small ice cream/cookie scoop drop dough on a greased cookie sheet.
  Sprinkle remaining 3 tablespoons (15 g) oats over tops.
- Bake for about 15 minutes, or until bottoms are golden and center feels firm. Let
  sit on baking sheet for 1 minute, then remove to a flat surface to cool completely.
- To make the maple glaze: Mix together the glaze ingredients, adding more sugar
  or rice milk until you reach the desired consistency. With a spoon, drizzle the glaze
  over the tops of the scones and let cool completely.

Yield: 3 dozen

Very Berry Mini Scones

These are so delicious. Whenever I have guests over I whip these up and they are always amazed that they are made without your usual ingredients. These are best eaten the day you make them (which is not hard to do!).

¼ cup (50 g) superfine sugar

¼ cup (60 g) unsweetened applesauce

¼ cup (50 g) Spectrum Organic Shortening

2 teaspoons (9.2 g) baking powder

Dash of salt

1 teaspoon (5 ml) vanilla extract

1½ cups (185 g) Bob's Red Mill white rice flour

½ cup (65 g) cornstarch (contains corn; can use tapioca or arrowroot starch instead)

½ cup (120 ml) rice milk or safe milk alternative

1 teaspoon (1.7 g) lemon zest (optional)

1 cup (145 g) fresh blueberries, raspberries, blackberries, or sliced strawberries (or a combination)

Raw sugar

DIRECTIONS

- Preheat oven to 375°F (190°C, or gas mark 5).
- With a mixer, combine the sugar and the next 9 ingredients (through zest, if using) and mix on low. Increase speed to medium for 1 minute. Stir in the berries.
- Use a medium ice cream/cookie scoop and drop dough on a greased cookie sheet or divide dough into two pieces and form into balls. Place one dough ball on a flat surface. Use a rolling pin to flatten dough into a thick round disk. Cut dough into 8 mini triangles (like pie or pizza slices).
- Place about 6 to 8 scones on a greased baking sheet or a baking sheet lined with nonstick parchment paper or aluminum foil. Sprinkle with raw sugar or brush with additional rice milk.
- Bake for about 25 to 30 minutes, or until bottoms are golden and centers feel firm to the touch. Let sit on baking sheet for 1 minute. Remove to a flat surface to cool. Best served warm.

Yield: 16 scones

Choco-nana Mini Scones

This is a hearty biscuit-type scone.

¼ cup (50 g) superfine sugar

⅔ cup (80 g) unsweetened applesauce

¼ cup (50 g) Spectrum Organic Shortening

2 teaspoons (9.6 g) baking powder

Dash of salt

1 teaspoon (5 ml) vanilla extract

2 cups (250 g) Bob's Red Mill white rice flour

½ cup (65 g) cornstarch (contains corn; can use tapioca or arrowroot starch instead)

½ cup (120 ml) rice milk or safe milk alternative

1 cup (80 g) certified gluten-free rolled oats

3 (1.4 ounce, or 40 g) Enjoy Life boom CHOCO boom dark chocolate bars chopped into 1-inch (2.5 cm) chunks

1 banana, cut into small chunks

DIRECTIONS

- Preheat oven to 375°F (190°C, or gas mark 5).
- With a mixer, combine sugar and next 8 ingredients (through rice milk) and mix on low. Increase speed to medium for 1 minute. Stir in oats, then the chocolate chunks and banana.
- Use a medium ice cream/cookie scoop and drop dough on a greased cookie sheet.
- Bake for about 15 minutes, or until bottoms are golden. Let sit on baking sheet for 1 minute. If desired, decorate with melted chocolate.

Yield: 16 scones

TIP FOR MESS-FREE DECORATION

Open a resealable plastic bag and place it in a small cup (like a child's sippy cup), then roll the edges over the lip of the cup. Secure in place with a rubber band. Now you can easily pour your melted chocolate, frosting, or other decoration into the plastic bag! Remove the rubber band, squeeze mixture into a corner of the bag, and cut off the tip. You are ready to decorate with hardly a mess.

Jammin' Mini Scones

¼ cup (50 g) superfine sugar

¼ cup (60 g) unsweetened applesauce

¼ cup (50 g) Spectrum Organic Shortening

2 teaspoons (9.2 g) baking powder

Dash of salt

1 teaspoon (5 ml) vanilla extract

½ cup (60 g) Bob's Red Mill white or brown rice flour

½ cup (56 g) flax meal

½ cup (50 g) certified gluten-free oat flour or rice bran

½ cup (60 g) Bob's Red Mill tapioca flour

½ cup (120 ml) rice milk or safe milk alternative

1 cup (320 g) your choice safe jam or jelly, such as strawberry, raspberry, grape, etc.

Raw or powdered sugar (contains cornstarch; can use corn-free recipe on page 43)

DIRECTIONS

- Preheat oven to 375°F (190°C, or gas mark 5).
- With a mixer, combine sugar and next 10 ingredients (through rice milk) and mix on low. Increase speed to medium for 1 minute.
- Divide dough into two balls. Place one dough ball on a flat surface. Use a rolling pin to flatten dough into a thick round disk. With a very sharp knife, carefully cut dough horizontally in half (like you would for a layer cake). Carefully remove the top. Spread ½ cup (160 g) of the jam over the bottom half of the dough. Cover with the top half. Repeat with other dough ball.
- Cut dough discs into 8 triangles (like pie or pizza slices).
- Brush tops with additional rice milk. Place about 6 to 8 scones on a greased baking sheet or a baking sheet lined with nonstick parchment paper or aluminum foil.
- Bake for about 15 to 20 minutes, or until bottoms are golden. Let sit on baking sheet for 1 minute to cool. Sprinkle raw sugar or sift powdered sugar over the tops.

Yield: 8 scones

Mini Chocolate Crisp Bites

These look like mini brownies at first glance, but when you take a bite you get a chocolaty crunch like a candy. These are quite lovely frosted. I make little flower decorations on the tops of each.

FOR COOKIES

10 ounces (280 g) Enjoy Life semi-sweet chocolate chips

3 cups (80 g) Enjoy Life Perky's "Nutty" Rice or small-shaped cereal

FOR FROSTING

1/4 cup (50 g) Spectrum Organic Shortening

1 teaspoon (5 ml) vanilla extract

2 cups (240 g) powdered sugar (contains cornstarch; can use corn-free recipe on page 43)

1 tablespoon (15 ml) water

Dash of salt

DIRECTIONS

- To make the cookies: Place chocolate chips in a large microwave-safe bowl. Microwave on medium heat at 30-second intervals, stirring at each interval, until melted and smooth. Stir in cereal with a wooden spoon and coat evenly.
- Grease a mini muffin pan. Use a small ice cream/cookie scoop to drop balls of mixture into each cup of the pan. Flatten (wet your hands to help prevent sticking, if desired).
- Place in the refrigerator to chill. When firm and chilled use a small knife to remove each cookie. Set on a flat surface.
- To make the frosting: In a food processor, combine all frosting ingredients. Blend until smooth. Decorate cookies with frosting.

Yield: 2 dozen

Berry Top Brownie Torte

Great for any party!

FOR TORTE

$1/2$ cup (125 g) unsweetened
  applesauce

2 tablespoons (30 ml) vegetable oil

1 cup (200 g) superfine sugar

$1/4$ teaspoon (1.5 g) salt

1 cup (175 g) Enjoy Life semi-sweet
  chocolate chips

1 teaspoon (5 ml) vanilla extract

$1/3$ cup (29 g) unsweetened cocoa

$1/4$ cup (60 ml) water

$1 1/2$ cups (185 g) Bob's Red Mill white
  or brown rice flour

$1/3$ cup (42 g) Bob's Red Mill
  tapioca flour

$1/2$ teaspoon (2.3 g) baking soda

FOR FROSTING

$1/4$ cup (50 g) Spectrum
  Organic Shortening

1 teaspoon (5 ml) vanilla extract

2 cups (240 g) powdered sugar
  (contains cornstarch; can use
  corn-free recipe on page 43)

1 tablespoon (15 ml) water

Dash of salt

FOR TOPPING

1 cup (110 g) fresh raspberries

1 cup (110 g) fresh strawberries, sliced

$1/2$ cup (70 g) fresh blueberries
  or blackberries

DIRECTIONS

- Preheat oven to 350°F (180°C, or gas mark 4).
- To make the torte: In a large saucepan combine, applesauce, oil, sugar, salt, chocolate chips, vanilla, cocoa, and water. Cook over low heat, stirring constantly, until chocolate chips are melted. Remove from heat. Stir in remaining torte ingredients. Pour into a greased 9-inch (23-cm) springform pan.
- Bake for about 25 minutes, or until slightly soft in the center and more firm around the edges. Let cool completely.
- To make the frosting: Combine all the frosting ingredients in a food processor and pulse until smooth.
- Frost cooled torte.
- Layer strawberries, blueberries, and raspberries over the top. Sprinkle with cinnamon, if desired. Remove the rim of the pan, cut into wedges, and serve.

Yield: 12 slices

Oh-So-Easy "Ice Cream" Sandwiches

This is a great treat for a kid's party.

1 ½ cups (210 g) safe ice cream alternative, softened

12 Enjoy Life cookies, such as Lively Lemon, Double Chocolate Brownie, or Happy Apple

DIRECTIONS

- Line a baking sheet with nonstick parchment paper or aluminum foil.
- With a small ice cream/cookie scoop, place one scoop of ice cream on the parchment paper.
- Semi-flatten 6 of the cookies. They will be the bases of the ice cream sandwiches. Position 2 cookies (1 flat cookie and 1 regular) with their flat sides facing the scooped ice cream ball, and press the two cookies firmly around the ice cream.
- Use a small spatula to smooth the ice cream around the rims of the cookies, filling in the edges. Immediately place in the freezer until ready to eat.

Yield: 6 sandwiches

Pumpkin Pie Pick-Ups

2 tablespoons (14 g) flax meal

1 ½ cups (355 ml) rice milk or safe milk alternative

2 teaspoons (9.2 g) baking powder

¾ cup (150 g) superfine sugar

½ cup (60 g) Bob's Red Mill white or brown rice flour

2 cups (490 g) canned pumpkin

1 teaspoon (5 ml) vanilla extract

½ teaspoon (3 g) salt

2 teaspoons (3.4 g) pumpkin pie spice (or make your own; see page 42)

¼ cup (25 g) powdered sugar (optional)

DIRECTIONS

- Preheat oven to 350°F (180°C, or gas mark 4).
- Place all ingredients except powdered sugar in a blender and purée for about 2 minutes. Pour into a greased 9-inch (23-cm) springform or pie pan.
- Bake for 35 minutes, or until the top and edges are browned, and the center is soft but cooked.
- Let cool. Remove springform pan rim. Slice into wedges. Sprinkle with powdered sugar, if desired.

Yield: 2 dozen

Chapter 8

Lite Bites: Healthy Cookies, Bars, and Bite-Size Treats

Try these treats when you are looking for a
yummy goodie that is low in added sugars and
is made with heartier flours.

Rice and Shine Balls

This is a healthy, quick, and easy treat to make. Have your kids help you roll the mixture into balls.

2 cups (520 g) sunflower butter or pumpkin butter

³/₄ cup (180 ml) firm honey

3 cups (300 g) allergy-friendly rice flakes or quinoa flakes

DIRECTIONS

- Mix together the sunflower butter and honey. Stir in the rice flakes. Roll into small balls. You may roll the balls in additional rice flakes, if desired.
- Refrigerate before eating.

Yield: 3 dozen

Perky's "Nutty" Power Bars

This recipe comes from the back of the box of the Enjoy Life Perky's "Nutty" Flax cereal (one of my favorites). It is an easy snack—give it a try.

1 cup (260 g) sunflower butter

¹/₂ cup (120 ml) brown rice syrup

¹/₂ teaspoon (2.5 ml) vanilla extract

¹/₈ teaspoon (0.8 g) salt

1 box (12 ounce, or 340-g) Enjoy Life Perky's "Nutty" Flax Cereal

¹/₄ cup (45 g) Enjoy Life semi-sweet chocolate chips

DIRECTIONS

- In a saucepan over medium-low heat, melt the sunflower butter, rice syrup, and vanilla until smooth.
- Combine remaining ingredients in a large bowl. Add sunflower butter mixture and stir to coat well.
- Press into a greased 8-inch (20-cm) square pan. Let cool before slicing.

Yield: 2 dozen

Breakfast to Go Squares

These squares are easy and have no added sugar.
This is a great breakfast treat on the go.

2 cups (340 g) quinoa flakes or steel-cut certified gluten-free oats

1 cup (175 g) packed dried sulfite-free apricots or apple pieces, chopped

DIRECTIONS

- Cook quinoa or oats according to package directions until very soft. Stir in dried fruit pieces.
- Pour mixture into a greased 8-inch (20-cm) square baking dish. Smooth top evenly. Let cool completely in the refrigerator until firm.
- Cut into 1-inch (2.5-cm) square pieces. Refrigerate until chilled.

Yield: 2 dozen

Heat's Off Chocolates

The raw food movement is becoming more popular. Although raw foods are often free of dairy, eggs, and gluten, do watch out because foods that are part of that movement often contain nuts.

3 tablespoons (38 g) Spectrum Organic Shortening or (45 ml) vegetable oil

²/₃ cup (117 g) sulfite-free dried prunes or date paste

¹/₃ cup (50 g) sulfite-free raisins

6 tablespoons (32 g) unsweetened cocoa powder

DIRECTIONS

- In a food processor, blend together all ingredients. Roll into little balls and place on a flat surface. Refrigerate.

Yield: 2 dozen

Feel-Good Fruit 'n Flax Cookies

*These are surprisingly good little biscuit cookies. You may add a
teaspoon of ground cinnamon or orange zest, if desired.*

1 cup (245 g) unsweetened
applesauce

1/2 cup (120 ml) pure maple syrup

2 cups (250 g) Bob's Red Mill white
or brown rice flour

1/2 cup (56 g) flax meal

1 teaspoon (6 g) salt

1 teaspoon (4.6 g) baking soda

1 teaspoon (4.6 g) baking powder

1 1/2 cups (245 g) packed sulfite-
free raisins, dates, or other dried
fruit pieces

2 teaspoons (5 g) flax seeds

DIRECTIONS

- Preheat oven to 350°F (180°C, or gas mark 4).
- With a mixer, stir together the applesauce and syrup. Add the flour and the
  next 4 ingredients (through baking powder) and blend well. Stir in the dried
  fruit and flaxseeds.
- Drop by 2-inch (5-cm) mounds onto a greased cookie sheet.
- Bake for about 15 minutes or until firm. Cool completely on the baking sheet.

Yield: 2 dozen

Honey Bunny Drops

A not-so-sweet treat!

¼ cup (50 g) Spectrum Organic Shortening

½ cup (125 g) unsweetened applesauce

½ cup (170 g) honey

1 teaspoon (5 ml) vanilla extract

1 ½ cups (185 g) Bob's Red Mill white rice flour

½ cup (60 g) Bob's Red Mill tapioca flour

2 teaspoons (9.2 g) baking powder

½ teaspoon (3 g) salt

1 cup (120 g) grated carrots

½ cup (75 g) sulfite-free golden raisins

DIRECTIONS

- Preheat oven to 375°F (190°C, or gas mark 5).
- Cream together shortening, applesauce, honey, and vanilla with a mixer. Add flours, baking powder, and salt and mix to combine. Stir in grated carrots and raisins.
- Drop dough by rounded tablespoon onto a greased baking sheet.
- Bake for 15 minutes. Remove from baking sheet and let cool on a flat surface.

Yield: About 2 dozen

Rice Ball Treats

Big and small kids like these. They are easy to make!

1 ³/₄ cups (415 ml) water

1 cup (195 g) short-grain brown or
   white rice

2 teaspoons (4.6 g) ground cinnamon

Dash of salt

¹/₄ cup (85 g) honey or (60 ml)
   pure maple syrup

1 cup (150 g) Enjoy Life Not Nuts!
   Beach Bash trail mix

DIRECTIONS

- In a saucepan, combine water, rice, cinnamon, salt, and honey. Cover and cook for about 40 minutes or until rice is very soft. Remove from heat and let stand, covered, for about 10 minutes. Stir in the trail mix. Transfer to a bowl and let cool for about 20 minutes, stirring occasionally.
- With damp hands, shape mixture into 1½-inch (3.7-cm) balls. Place on a flat surface. Eat warm or enjoy chilled from the refrigerator.

Yield: 3 dozen

Fab Fruit, Flax, and Quinoa Drops

These are yummy little cookies. Quinoa delivers the flavor.

1/3 cup (80 ml) vegetable oil

1/2 cup (170 g) honey

1 teaspoon (5 ml) vanilla extract

1/2 cup (56 g) flax meal

1/4 cup (32 g) cornstarch (contains corn; can use tapioca or arrowroot starch instead)

2 cups (200 g) quinoa flakes

1 teaspoon (4.6 g) baking powder

1/4 cup (60 ml) water

1 cup (150 g) Enjoy Life Not Nuts! Mountain Mambo or Beach Bash trail mix

DIRECTIONS

- Preheat oven to 350°F (180°C, or gas mark 4).
- Mix the oil, honey, and vanilla. Add the flax, starch, quinoa flakes, and baking powder and mix on low speed. With mixer on low, slowly pour in the water until the dough is smooth. Stir in the trail mix.
- Use a small ice cream/cookie scoop or drop by tablespoon onto a baking sheet, spacing the cookies about 2 inches (5 cm) apart (about 6 cookies per baking sheet). Flatten with a spatula.
- Bake for about 12 to 15 minutes, or until golden around the edges and soft in the center. For softer cookies, remove from oven before they get too golden—around 12 minutes. Let cool on baking sheet for less than 1 minute. Remove with a flat spatula and place on a flat surface to cool completely.

Yield: 2 dozen

Apple Berry Bounty Bars

I created this recipe is for a friend in Canada who loved the Skip the Sugar Apricot Bars but doesn't really like apricots.

FOR PASTRY

1 cup (125 g) oat or sorghum flour

¼ cup (30 g) Bob's Red Mill brown rice flour

¼ cup (28 g) flax meal

¼ cup (25 g) teff flour or rice bran

⅓ cup (80 ml) vegetable oil

½ cup (120 ml) apple juice

Dash of salt

½ teaspoon (1.2 g) ground cinnamon

FOR APPLE BERRY FILLING

1 ⅓ cups (315 ml) apple juice

1 tablespoon (8 g) cornstarch (contains corn; can use tapioca or arrowroot starch instead)

1 teaspoon (2.3 g) ground cinnamon

1 cup (175 g) packed sulfite-free dried apple pieces

½ cup (70 g) fresh blueberries or raspberries

2 tablespoons (30 ml) rice milk, safe milk alternative, or apple juice

DIRECTIONS

- Preheat oven to 400°F (200°C, or gas mark 6).
- To make the pastry: In a food processor, combine all pastry ingredients and pulse until crumbly. Process until the mixture forms into a ball. Set aside.
- To make the filling: Whisk together apple juice, starch, and cinnamon in a saucepan. Stir in apples. Cook on medium heat for about 20 minutes. Turn off heat and let cool slightly. Stir in berries.
- Grease a 9 x 13-inch (23 x 33-cm) baking pan or a springform pan. Divide dough into two equal balls. Place one ball on a piece of nonstick parchment paper or plastic wrap and cover with an additional piece of parchment paper or plastic wrap. With a rolling pin, roll dough into a thin rectangle or disc the size of your prepared pan. Repeat with second dough ball and set aside.
- Place the first dough piece into the pan and press in firmly. Cut off excess dough around the edges.
- Pour the apple berry mixture into a blender or food processor and purée into a paste. Spread the apple paste over the top of the dough in the pan.
- Lay the second dough piece over the top of the apple berry mixture. Flatten slightly. Push dough into corners to seal the bars. Cut off excess dough around edges, if needed.
- Brush the top of the bars with rice milk or apple juice. Prick the top of the pastry with a fork.
- Bake for about 30 to 40 minutes, or until bars are firm when tapped. Let cool completely. Cut into squares or bars.

Yield: 2 dozen

Skip the Sugar Apricot Bars

*Do you want a fabulous treat with no added sugar? This is the cookie for you!
Plenty of flavor is packed into these little tasty bars.*

FOR PASTRY

1 cup (125 g) oat or sorghum flour

¼ cup (30 g) Bob's Red Mill brown
   rice flour

¼ cup (28 g) flax meal

¼ cup (25 g) teff flour or rice bran

⅓ cup (80 ml) vegetable oil

½ cup (120 ml) apple juice

Dash of salt

½ teaspoon (1.2 g) ground cinnamon

FOR APRICOT FILLING

1 cup (175 g) packed sulfite-free
   dried apricots

1 ⅓ cups (315 ml) apple juice

1 teaspoon (2.3 g) ground cinnamon

⅓ cup (50 g) sulfite-free raisins

2 tablespoons (30 ml) rice milk, safe
   milk alternative, or apple juice

DIRECTIONS

- Preheat oven to 400°F (200°C, or gas mark 6).
- To make the pastry: In a food processor, combine all the pastry ingredients and pulse until crumbly. Process until the mixture forms into a ball. Set aside.
- To make the filling: Combine apricots, apple juice, and cinnamon in a saucepan. Cook over medium heat for about 20 minutes. Turn off heat and let cool slightly.
- Grease a 9 x 13-inch (23 x 33-cm) baking pan or a springform pan. Divide dough into two equal balls. Place one ball on a piece of nonstick parchment paper or plastic wrap and cover with an additional piece of parchment paper or plastic wrap. With a rolling pin, roll dough into a thin rectangle or disc the size of your prepared pan. Repeat with second dough ball.
- Place the first dough piece into the pan and press in firmly. Cut off excess dough around the edges.
- Pour the apricot mixture into a blender or food processor and purée into a paste. Stir in the raisins.
- Spread the apricot paste over the top of the dough in the pan.
- Lay the second dough piece over the top of the apricot mixture. Flatten slightly. Push dough into the corners to seal the bars. Cut off excess dough around the edges if needed.
- Brush the top of the bars with rice milk or apple juice. Prick the top of the pastry with a fork.
- Bake for about 30 to 40 minutes, or until firm when tapped. Let cool completely. Cut into squares or bars.

Yield: 2 dozen

Banana Bunch Drops

2 bananas, mashed

1/2 cup (120 ml) unsulfured molasses

2 cups (160 g) certified gluten-free
   rolled oats or rolled rice flakes

1/2 cup (60 g) Bob's Red Mill white or
   brown rice flour

1/2 cup (56 g) flax meal

1 teaspoon (4.6 g) baking soda

1/2 teaspoon (0.9 g) ground ginger

1/2 teaspoon (1.1 g) ground nutmeg

1/2 teaspoon (1.2 g) ground cinnamon

1/3 cup (50 g) sulfite-free raisins

DIRECTIONS

- Preheat oven to 350°F (180°C, or gas mark 4).
- In a food processor, cream together bananas and molasses. Add remaining ingredients and mix well. Drop by spoonfuls onto baking sheet.
- Bake for 15 minutes, or until lightly browned. Remove to a flat surface to cool.

Yield: 3 dozen

Power Balls

Made with seeds and fruits, this is a really fun treat.
Have the kids help you roll them into balls.

2 cups (290g) sunflower seed kernels

1 cup (165 g) packed sulfite-free
  raisins

½ cup (89 g) sulfite-free dates,
  chopped

2 apples, grated

2 large bananas, sliced

1 teaspoon (2.3 g) ground cinnamon

1 tablespoon (15 ml) vegetable oil

1 cup (112 g) flax meal or rice bran

DIRECTIONS

- In a food processor, add sunflower seeds, raisins, and dates and pulse until mixture is the consistency of flax meal. Add remaining ingredients and purée until you have a smooth paste.
- Pinch off desired amount of dough and roll into balls. Refrigerate until chilled.

Yield: 2 dozen

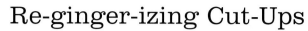

Re-ginger-izing Cut-Ups

*Have healthy fun with decorations on your gingerbread men—here,
trail mix provides the décor!*

½ cup (100 g) Spectrum
  Organic Shortening

¼ cup (60 g) packed brown sugar

½ cup (120 ml) unsulfured molasses

1 tablespoon (15 ml) vinegar

¼ cup (60 g) unsweetened
  applesauce

1 teaspoon (4.6 g) baking powder

1 teaspoon (1.8 g) ground ginger

½ teaspoon (2.3 g) baking soda

½ teaspoon (1.2 g) ground cinnamon

½ teaspoon (1 g) ground cloves

1 cup (125 g) Bob's Red Mill brown
  rice flour

½ cup (50 g) rice bran

½ cup (56 g) flax meal

½ cup (60 g) Bob's Red Mill
  tapioca flour

½ cup (75 g) your favorite Enjoy Life
  Not Nuts! trail mix

DIRECTIONS

- Preheat oven to 350°F (180°C, or gas mark 4).
- In a food processor, combine the shortening, brown sugar, molasses, vinegar, and applesauce until smooth. Add the baking powder and the next 8 ingredients (through tapioca flour) and process until the dough forms into a ball.
- Divide dough into fourths. Place one section of dough between two pieces of nonstick parchment paper. With a rolling pin, roll dough into a flat ½-inch (1.2 cm) thick disk.
- Cut shapes out of dough cookie cutters. Use a flat spatula to gently remove the cookies to a greased baking sheet. Collect remaining dough and repeat process.
- Bake for about 12 minutes (depending on size of cookie), or until the cookies are darker around the edges and firm in the centers. Remove with a spatula to a flat surface to cool.
- While cookies are warm, press pieces of the trail mix into each cookie. For example, to make one gingerbread man you could use 2 raisin eyes, a sunflower mouth, chocolate chip buttons, and pineapple pieces on his shoes.

Yield: 2 dozen

Sunny Honey Cookies

1 cup (125 g) Bob's Red Mill brown
 rice flour

1 tablespoon (7 g) flax meal

2 tablespoons (30 ml) vegetable oil

1/4 cup (85 g) honey

1/2 teaspoon (3 g) salt

1 teaspoon (5 ml) vanilla extract

1 cup (145 g) sunflower seed kernels,
 ground into a meal. Sunflower seeds
 for topping optional

DIRECTIONS

- Preheat oven to 350°F (180°C, or gas mark 4).
- Place all ingredients in a food processor and process until smooth. Pinch off
  1 teaspoon (5 g) of dough and roll into a ball. Place on cookie sheet and flatten
  slightly. Repeat with remaining dough.
- Bake for about 12 minutes, or until golden around the edges. Let sit for 1 minute,
  then remove with a spatula to a flat surface to cool completely.

Yield: 2 dozen

Oatmeal Bowl to Go

3 cups (240 g) certified gluten-free
  rolled oats

1 teaspoon (4.6 g) baking soda

1 teaspoon (6 g) salt

2 tablespoons (43 g) honey or pure
  maple syrup

2 tablespoons (30 ml) vegetable oil

½ cup (80 g) dried sulfite-free raisins,
  apples, apricots, or combination

½ cup (120 ml) water

2 teaspoons (10 ml) vanilla

½ cup (60 g) Bob's Red Mill brown
  rice flour

DIRECTIONS

- Preheat oven to 350°F (180°C, or gas mark 4).

- Mix all ingredients in a bowl and let sit for half an hour. Place mixture in a food processor and process until you have a thick dough. Scoop out dough with a small ice cream/cookie scoop and drop onto a greased baking sheet. Flatten each cookie.

- Bake for about 15 minutes or until firm. Let cool on the baking sheet for 2 minutes before removing to a flat surface to cool completely.

Yield: 2 dozen

Granola Bar One-Bites

2 tablespoons (30 ml) vegetable oil

2 tablespoons (30 g) brown sugar

2 tablespoons (43 g) honey

2 tablespoons (14 g) flax meal

2 tablespoons (30 ml) water

1 ripe banana, sliced

1 teaspoon (5 ml) vanilla extract

1/2 cup (60 g) Bob's Red Mill white or brown rice flour or sorghum flour

2 tablespoons (15 g) Bob's Red Mill tapioca flour

1 teaspoon (2.3 g) ground cinnamon

1 1/3 cups (140 g) Enjoy Life granola, any flavor

1 cup (150 g) Enjoy Life Not Nuts! trail mix, any flavor

DIRECTIONS

- Preheat oven to 350°F (180°C, or gas mark 4).
- With a mixer, cream together the first 7 ingredients (through vanilla). Mix in flours and cinnamon until smooth. Stir in granola and trail mix. If desired, place granola in a plastic bag and gently crush with a rolling pin into bite-size pieces. Spoon mixture into a greased 9-inch (23-cm) baking pan or greased mini muffin pan.
- Bake for 30 minutes if using the 9-inch (23-cm) baking pan or 20 minutes if using the mini muffin pan. Cool and cut into small bars or remove from muffin pan.

Yield: 2 dozen

Sunny Nature Snack Bites

A quick and simple treat for your family. An apple corer/slicer makes this yummy snack a cinch to make!

1 large apple or firm pear

⅓ cup (87 g) sunflower butter

1 cup (104 g) Enjoy Life granola, any flavor, crushed

DIRECTIONS

- Wash and core the apple. Cut the apple into 8 sections or wedges. Leave the peel on. Set apple wedges on a plate, peel side down.
- Spread a thin layer of sunflower butter on both sides of the apple wedge.
- Sprinkle with granola. Serve immediately.

Yield: 8 slices

Fancy-That Fruit

This is a fabulous dessert idea. Make it as simple or as fancy as you want.
Try bringing this to a child's classroom party—it is a guaranteed hit!

15 strawberries

1 cup (175 g) Enjoy Life semi-sweet
chocolate chips

¼ cup (50 g) safe candy, colored
sugar, or sprinkles for decorating

DIRECTIONS

- Wash and dry the strawberries. Keep the stems on.
- Melt chocolate in a microwave-safe bowl in 30-second intervals, stirring at each interval, until smooth. Let melted chocolate cool slightly and pour into a heavy-duty resealable plastic bag. Cut a small tip off one corner of the bag. Zigzag stripes of chocolate over each strawberry. Or pour melted chocolate into a bowl and dip each strawberry halfway in. Place on a cookie sheet lined with nonstick parchment paper. Sprinkle with candy, additional chocolate chips, or sprinkles, if desired.
- Refrigerate until ready to serve. Remove fruit from parchment paper and place on a serving plate.

Yield: 15 pieces

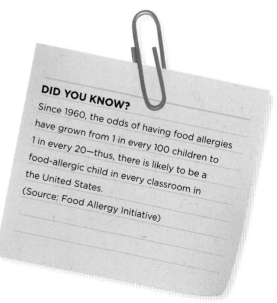

DID YOU KNOW?
Since 1960, the odds of having food allergies have grown from 1 in every 100 children to 1 in every 20—thus, there is likely to be a food-allergic child in every classroom in the United States.
(Source: Food Allergy Initiative)

Chapter 9

Resources

This is such a wonderful time for living with food allergies. I am always impressed with the knowledge and information that is available to the public on the Internet, in restaurants, with doctors, and with child-care providers. Food allergies and diseases that require you to change your diet are statistically on the rise, and awareness is increasing. Every day, doctors are learning more and more. When I was a kid I felt as if I was some sort of anti-food misfit. My friends, school, and family really didn't understand. Today, if I am in a restaurant or talking to the parents of my child's play date, I can say the word "celiac" or food allergies and they have heard of it, know someone with it, or are willing to follow the procedures to help protect my family from it.

Wow. What a great day and age!

It might be overwhelming when you hear that first diagnosis, but do realize, it does get easier. They say if you try something for thirty days it becomes a habit. Make yours a habit to stick to your "special diet" to stay happy and healthy!

If you are new to "special diets," find other families or online support groups to talk with and ask questions. Sometimes hearing stories and suggestions from others (who you can relate to) helps you put your situation into perspective. That is why I included a few stories and tips throughout this book from real people like you, who share their inspiration and advice. I am also including a list of helpful websites to connect you to the resources you need to help you and your family stay safe and healthy.

WHY ARE DEDICATED FACILITIES IMPORTANT?

Look for products that are made in dedicated facilities, meaning that they are not produced in facilities or on shared equipment with other allergen-containing foods. This significantly reduces the risk of mistakes. Although all food manufacturers should have good allergen control procedures in place, mistakes can still happen. You should know that all Enjoy Life products are made in a dedicated nut- and gluten-free facility for both your safety and peace of mind. If you or your families are affected by severe allergies, you should sign up to receive food recall alerts from www.recalls.gov or the Food Allergy and Anaphylaxis Network (www.foodallergy.org)

FINDING SPECIALTY INGREDIENTS

For information about where to find the specialty ingredients discussed in this book or simple recipes for making your own ingredients, please refer back to chapter 3, Stocking an Allergy-Friendly Kitchen, (pages 34–45). Specifically, for:

Flours and starches, see pages 38–39

Butter and egg substitutes, see page 40

Baking necessities, see pages 42–43

Sugars, see page 44

Other good stuff, see page 45

Helpful websites:

CELIAC DISEASE

American Celiac Disease Alliance (ACDA), www.americanceliac.org

Canadian Celiac Association (CCA), www.celiac.ca

Celiac.com, www.celiac.com

Chock full of information, gluten-free and wheat-free diet resources, and links to online stores.

Celiac Disease Center at Columbia University, www.celiacdiseasecenter.columbia.edu

Celiac Disease Foundation (CDF), www.celiac.org

Programs for disease awareness, education, advocacy, and research.

Celiac Sprue Association (CSA), www.csaceliacs.org

Regional support groups, safe foods list, newsletter, and phone and online resources.

Gluten-Free Certification Organization (GFCO), www.gfco.org

Independent certification organization for gluten-free foods. All Enjoy Life products are certified gluten-free by the GFCO.

Gluten-Free Living Magazine, www.glutenfreeliving.com

National magazine for people with Celiac Disease or gluten intolerance.

Glutenfreemall.com, www.glutenfreemall.com

Great online retailer with a broad selection of gluten-free and allergy-friendly foods and ingredients.

Gluten Intolerance Group of North America (GIG), www.gluten.net

Printable materials, support groups, newsletter, conferences, kids' camps, restaurant cards, and advocacy.

National Foundation for Celiac Awareness (NFCA), www.celiaccentral.org

Triumph Dining: Gluten-Free Restaurant Guide and Gluten-Free Grocery Guide, www.triumphdining.com *Working to make following a gluten-free diet easier.*

University of Chicago Celiac Disease Center, www.celiacdisease.net

Dedicated to raising diagnosis rates and meeting the critical needs of people affected by Celiac Disease through education, research, and advocacy. Talk to an expert about symptoms, testing, diagnosis, and procedures by calling 773.702.7593.

University of Maryland Center for Celiac Research, www.celiaccenter.org

FOOD ALLERGIES

Allergic Living Magazine, www.allergicliving.com

Canadian magazine for people with food and/or environmental allergies. Every issue is filled with great information, recipes, and more!

Allergygrocer.com, www.allergygrocer.com

Online store for people with food allergies.

Allergy Moms, www.allergymoms.com

Blog, resources, newsletter, and more.

Allerneeds.com, www.allerneeds.com

Online store with peanut- and tree nut–free snacks.

Anaphylaxis Canada, www.anaphylaxis.ca

Helpful resources for Canadians affected by food allergies and anaphylaxis.

Eat, Learn, Live, www.ellfoundation.org

Dedicated to enabling food-allergic children to eat, learn, and live safely.

Food Allergy and Anaphylaxis Network (FAAN), www.foodallergy.org

Pamphlets, resources, research, advocacy, kids and teen sites and more!

Food Allergy Initiative (FAI), www.foodallergyinitiative.org

Funds research and programs for awareness, education, and advocacy.

Godairyfree.com, www.godairyfree.com

Great resource on how to cook, shop, and dine dairy-free.

Kids with Food Allergies (KFA), www.kidswithfoodallergies.org

Very helpful discussion forum, resources, and newsletter.

Living Without Magazine, www.livingwithout.com

National magazine for people with food allergies/sensitivities and Celiac Disease. Great resource for recipes and information!

Peanutfreeplanet.com, www.peanutfreeplanet.com

Online store for people with peanut allergies.

AUTISM AND GFCF DIET

Autism Network for Dietary Intervention (ANDI), www.autismndi.com

Help with dietary intervention strategies for parents of autistic children.

Autism Research Institute/Defeat Autism Now (DAN), www.autism.com

The latest research, information, and conferences on autism.

Autism Society of America, www.autism-society.org

Information, resources, Autism Advocate magazine and advocacy.

Autism Society of Canada, www.autismsocietycanada.ca

Information, research, and resources for Canadian families affected by autism.

Gluten-Free Casein-Free Diet Support Group, www.gfcfdiet.com

Events, discussion forum, links, and a newsletter for people following a GFCF diet.

Talk about Curing Autism (TACA), www.tacanow.com

Information, resources, and support for families affected by autism.

ACKNOWLEDGMENTS

Thank you to my publishing company. A special thank you to Jill Alexander, you have been a great editor and a special friend. Will, thank you for all your help! A big thank you to all the ELF'ers! Of course, thank you to my mom, dad, brothers, and my Jen's, Beth, Jan and Jenny, and Chris.

—Leslie Hammond

Thank you to my husband Perttu, and my two beautiful daughters Anne and Maggie for their encouragement, support, and use of their "taste buds." Thanks Leslie for your very creative work with the recipes and your upbeat attitude amidst the deadlines. Thank you to my friend, Auli, for your help with testing and tasting the recipes, it was really appreciated. Thank you Nancy Curby for all time you spent on reviewing the details and making sure everything ran smoothly for Enjoy Life, you are such a great attribute to this book. Thank you Scott Mandell for starting Enjoy Life and all the people your company has helped. And thanks to the many tasters from Enjoy Life, Creative Care, family, and friends. Lastly, I would like to thank everyone at Fair Winds Press – especially Jill Alexander and John Gettings for this opportunity. It was fun!

—Betsy Laakso

About the Authors

LESLIE HAMMOND is a culinary expert who focuses on allergies and allergy-free goods. She volunteers her time to educate the public and create awareness about alternative eating. She is the coauthor of the Kid-Friendly Food Allergy Cookbook. She lives in northern California.

BETSY LAAKSO is director of research and development for Enjoy Life Natural Brands, which was founded in 2001 with the mission of making great-tasting allergy-friendly foods that most everyone can eat freely. The company launched the Enjoy Life brand in 2002 with a product line that is free of the eight most common allergens and gluten-free.

Index